TREATMENT AND PREVENTION OF CHILDHOOD SEXUAL ABUSE

TREATMENT AND PREVENTION OF CHILDHOOD SEXUAL ABUSE
A Child-Generated Model

Sandra A. Burkhardt, Ph.D.
Anthony F. Rotatori, Ph.D.
Saint Xavier University
Chicago, Illinois

Taylor & Francis
Publishers since 1798

USA	Publishing Office:	Taylor & Francis
		1101 Vermont Avenue, N.W., Suite 200
		Washington, DC 20005-3521
		Tel: (202) 289-2174
		Fax: (202) 289-3665
	Distribution Center:	Taylor & Francis
		1900 Frost Road, Suite 101
		Bristol, PA 19007-1598
		Tel: (215) 785-5800
		Fax: (215) 785-5515
UK		Taylor & Francis Ltd.
		4 John St.
		London WC1N 2ET
		Tel: 071 405 2237
		Fax: 071 831 2035

TREATMENT AND PREVENTION OF CHILDHOOD SEXUAL ABUSE:
A Child-Generated Model

1 2 3 4 5 6 7 8 9 0   BRBR   9 8 7 6 5

This book was set in Times Roman by Harlowe Typography, Inc. The editor was Heather Jefferson. Prepress supervisor was Miriam Gonzalez. Cover design by Michelle M. Fleitz. Printing and binding by Braun-Brumfield, Inc.

A CIP catalog record for this book is available from the British Library.

∞ The paper in this publication meets the requirements of the ANSI Standard Z39.48-1984 (Permanence of Paper)

Library of Congress Cataloging-in-Publication Data
Burkhardt, Sandra A.
    Treatment and prevention of child sexual abuse : a child-generated
model / by Sandra A. Burkhardt, Anthony F. Rotatori.
        p. cm.
    Includes bibliographical references.

    1. Sexually abused children—Psychology.   2. Child sexual abuse—
Prevention.   3. Sexually abused children—Rehabilitation.
4. Children and adults.   5. Attribution (Social psychology) in
children.   I. Rotatori, Anthony F.   II. Title.
RJ507.S49B87   1995
618.92'85836—dc20   95-7942
                                                        CIP

ISBN 1-56032-320-5

Contents

Foreword

Although professionals in the child sexual abuse area have long known that children have personal, physical, and emotional characteristics that heighten their vulnerability to child sexual abuse, this volume clearly demonstrates that there are also vulnerabilities associated with how children normally think, interpret, and problem solve. As such, this work fills a gap in the existing literature on child sexual abuse, and is likely to be invaluable to both clinicians and researchers who work in the area of child sexual abuse.

In this volume, the reader finds something rare—a true integration of science and practice. The authors have compiled a scholarly work in which they describe a developmental perspective on childhood vulnerability to sexual victimization. As a researcher and a clinician in the area of child sexual abuse for some 20 years, I have often been frustrated that the worlds of science and practice are often found in different volumes. This book was rewarding for me because I was not left to provide my own interpretation of how research and intervention are connected. The authors provide a readable summary of the cognitive developmental and social cognitive developmental literatures as they are relevant to the area of child sexual abuse. The authors interviewed many children and, true to their own pleas to other professionals to "listen to the children's own words," they let the children tell us how to view threatening situations from a child's perspective. Implications are clearly made about how to educate children about child sexual abuse, how to develop prevention programming, and how to plan clinical interventions once abuse has been identified. This volume is truly a magnificent example of scholarship and clinical wisdom, full of valuable ideas for both novice and experienced professionals in the field of child sexual abuse.

Sheila C. Ribordy, Ph.D.
De Paul University

Preface

The reporting of child sexual abuse has increased 200% since 1976. Prevention and treatment of this problem are key concerns for parents and professionals. The stakes are also high for children. Early victimization may result in the disturbance, delay, or derailing of normal social cognitive development, with victims at risk for involvement in dangerous or abusive relationships into adulthood. A child-generated model of sexual abuse intervention identifies the characteristics of children's reasoning about perpetrators for the purpose of determining useful prevention strategies and appropriate treatment goals.

The need for this information can be attested to by the numerous books that have appeared on the market in the past 10 years; the extensive coverage of the topic by local and national newspapers, television, and radio news programs; and the proliferation of courses, workshops, and inservice training for mental health practitioners. Initially, the expert-based information on child sexual abuse presented to professionals during the 1980s included factual and theoretical aspects of abuse indicators, treatment techniques, and statutory child-care procedures. More recently, field-initiated developmental interventions based on child victimization research have enhanced the earlier theoretical works. Furthermore, treating professionals' recognition of a need for child-generated information models to treat and prevent childhood sexual abuse is dominating the field and becoming the intervention of choice.

This practitioner-oriented book presents a child-generated therapeutic model of intervention that guides educators and mental health professionals to: (a) acquire information about what and how children think about adults, in general, and perpetrators, in particular; (b) inventory children's strategies for responding to perpetrators; (c) document children's underlying logic for the strategies they identify; and (d) use the information provided by children to guide the selection of techniques for prevention and treatment of sexual abuse.

The model is based on empirical research concerned with the established correlates of child sexual abuse. The cornerstone of the book is that effective prevention and therapeutic strategies must emphasize child-generated information that points out to the clinician how typical children think. This information allows the clinician to assess and understand the vulnerability of sexually abused children or adults, in comparison with the cognitive understanding and emotional reactions of unmolested children. The approach differs from earlier traditional models of intervention, which rely on adult conceptualizations such as ''Just say no and go.'' Although adults believe these cognitive strategies to be effective, children may not have the capability to fully utilize the strategies to prevent or stop the abuse. Furthermore, it is critical for a practitioner to understand that children exhibit individual reactions and coping strategies in the face of victimization based on their gender and level of development.

The book is composed of six chapters and an appendix. Chapter 1 provides an introduction to the topic of child sexual abuse. Specifically, it includes: the definition of, prevalence of, and vulnerability to child sexual abuse; how adults view childhood sexual abuse; prevention efforts; characteristics of perpetrators; and ways to help victims. Chapter 2 provides a comprehensive discussion of the correlates of child sexual abuse. Topics covered include: theoretical models of victim vulnerability; the relationship among cognitive, developmental, and socioemotional factors and sexual abuse; and the importance of the child's view of authority and interpersonal understanding as it relates to being victimized. Chapter 3 presents detailed information on a systematic research endeavor into victim vulnerability. The content of the chapter includes: a rationale of the association between a child's level of social reasoning and his or her vulnerability to childhood sexual abuse, a critical examination of factors of vulnerability, a discussion of the goals of a child-generated method of sexual abuse intervention, a description of the Perpetrator Interview, procedures to analyze interview data, and insightful discourse on children's resistance and reporting strategies. Chapter 4 describes how children respond to perpetrators. Included is information about recognition of perpetrators, how boys and girls of different ages respond to perpetrators, group data that identify children most at risk, and actual clinical descriptions of children's responses to the Perpetrator Interview. Chapter 5 presents the Burkhardt child-generated model of sexual abuse intervention. The chapter includes: the model's principles; how children fail to recognize perpetrators; ways to improve recognition, resistance, and reporting; implications for prevention and treatment; and future research needs. Chapter 6 provides procedures to assess child sexual abuse. Its content includes: terminology, categories, and occurrence of child sexual abuse; symptoms and variables related to child sexual abuse; data collection, testing, and interview procedures that should be utilized; and a format for integrating the assessment data and establishing a hierarchical model for evaluation. Finally, an appendix provides a description of educational and psychological materials on childhood sexual abuse that can be used for intervention.

The book's primary audience is mental health counselors, teachers, nurses, social workers, psychologists, and psychiatrists who provide prevention consultation and therapeutic intervention for sexually abused children and adult survivors. A secondary audience is graduate students who are enrolled in counseling courses, practicum, or internship training concerned with children. A final audience is university professors who teach courses in which childhood sexual abuse is covered.

The authors wish to acknowledge the significant contribution of Mary Kaley to the research and writing of chapter 1, the contributions of Kirsten Solfisburg and Julie Kosier to the writing of chapter 6, and the work of Trish Smith, Ph.D., in compiling the appendix. A special thanks to Mary Ann Murphy and Marlin Hoover, Ph.D., for their assistance in data and manuscript preparation, as well as their kind encouragement of the authors; to Linda Camras, Ph.D., and Mari Brown, Ph.D., for useful suggestions regarding research design; to Larry Chambers, Ph.D., and Algis Norvilas, Ph.D., of St. Xavier University for supporting the authors' time commitment to the project; to James Burkhardt and Rocco and Sandi Cardillo for computer assistance; to research assistants Diane Mercer, Jane Bylina, Colleen Farrell, Diana Schubert, Tom Slazyk, Marybeth Spitzer, and Judy Wojchiechowski; and to the parents, teachers, administrators, and children who made the interviews possible.

A personal thank you to Mary and Carl Mazzoni for a lifetime of loving care; to Dale Burkhardt, for providing emotional as well as financial support for both the Burkhardt study and the researcher; and to Vikki Burkhardt, the inspiration for wanting to keep all children precious and safe.

Chapter 1

Toward an Understanding of Childhood Sexual Abuse

Even as the question Why are children sexually abused? remains unanswered, caring adults are eager to understand how children are victimized. Identifying the complex psychological, social, and physical factors that contribute to children's vulnerability to sexual abuse may be essential to successful prevention and treatment efforts. Understanding childhood sexual abuse may begin with defining abuse, but rapidly mobilizes a desire to halt that which is being defined.

Aimed at promoting and preserving public health, sexual abuse interventions, like other prevention efforts, can be categorized as *primary*, *secondary*, and *tertiary* prevention (Felner, Jason, Moritsugu, & Farber, 1983; Goldston, 1977). Primary prevention of childhood sexual abuse involves preventing abuse from happening in the first place. Secondary prevention includes early detection and reporting of perpetrators for the purpose of stopping the perpetrator and minimizing negative effects for the child. Tertiary intervention focuses on the treatment of abused children and adults who have developed signs and symptoms of distress. In general, prevention programs, such as school-based "stranger awareness" presentations and reporting hotlines, are aimed at primary and secondary prevention. Professional and self-help therapies, such as individual psychotherapy, support groups for incest survivors, and residential programs for offenders, are examples of tertiary care.

Prevention of childhood sexual abuse has proved a difficult task with unreliable outcomes (Daro, 1991; Melton, 1992b; Pelcovitz, Adler, Kaplan, Packman, & Krieger, 1992). Treatment of victims and perpetrators, based on a range of theories and opinions, has proceeded without consensus regarding the therapeutic goals to be achieved and the methods to be employed. Effective treatment of perpetrators has not been reliably accomplished (Furniss, 1991), and clinical populations include substantial numbers of adults who were sexually abused as children (Green, 1993). These findings suggest a pressing social need to better understand childhood sexual abuse.

Both the popular press and professional literature are filled with surveys, studies, and speculations about the causes, effects, and implications of childhood sexual abuse. Recent developments regarding retrieval of repressed/false memories, celebrity disclosures of childhood sexual abuse, and horrid headlines of murder and mayhem have pitted parents against their adult children, therapists against family members, and professionals against each other. Challenges and debates regarding society's awareness of and response to childhood sexual abuse have emerged (Olafson, Corwin, & Summit, 1993). Disputes over the veracity of victims' reports, the use of unproved treatment methods such as hypnosis, and the possibility that childhood sexual abuse provides legal justification for the killing of the perpetrator remain unresolved (e.g., Goldstein, 1992; Yapko, 1993).

Amid the adult posturing, the children's views are seldom heard. A child-generated model of sexual abuse intervention studies the phenomenon of childhood sexual abuse from the child's perspective. A child-generated model maintains that understanding how children reason about themselves and perpetrators is essential to effective prevention and treatment of sexual abuse. In contrast to models that stem from adults' ideas and observations about what children should know, a child-generated model seeks to understand what a child *can* know. Understanding sexual abuse from a child's perspective begins with an overview of the terms and concepts associated with childhood sexual abuse.

DEFINING CHILDHOOD SEXUAL ABUSE

In 1978, the National Center on Child Abuse and Neglect (NCCAN) defined *childhood sexual abuse* as follows:

> Contacts or interactions between a child and an adult when the child is being used for the sexual stimulation of the perpetrator or another person. Sexual abuse may also be committed by a person under the age of 18 when that person is either significantly older than the victim or when the perpetrator is in a position of power or control over another's child. (p. 2)

This definition of childhood sexual abuse includes a variety of activities perpetrated by relatives (intrafamilial abuse) or unrelated adults (extrafamilial abuse), such as strangers, neighbors, community helpers, or friends. Definitions of specific sexually abusive activities, including *exhibitionism, child pornography*, and *child prostitution*, appear in chapter 6. Yet beyond technical definitions of who is doing what to whom is the implication that children are vulnerable to perpetrators in psychological as well as physical ways.

The NCCAN definition notes that a child "is being used." Wurtele and Miller-Perrin (1992) observed that " . . . sexual abuse involves the exploitation of children's ignorance, trust, and obedience" (pp. 5–6). Thus, one would expect to find children's reactions to perpetrators filled with confusion, mislaid loyalty, and automatic compliance with authority figures. If, as Wurtele and Miller-Perrin maintained, definitions of childhood sexual abuse are "culture-bound" and "direct reflections of the values and orientations of communities and societies at large" (p. 3), one would expect children's views of sexual abuse to reflect a "subculture of childhood" characterized by knowledge, beliefs, actions, values, and hopes shared by most children.

How are children to develop an understanding of sexual abuse? For example, sexual abuse is frequently referred to as "bad touch," with little or no emphasis on the sexual nature of sexual abuse (Finkelhor & Strapko, 1992; Melton, 1992a). Children may be unaware that the physical contact associated with "bad touch" is considered "bad" because it is stimulating to the perpetrator (Wurtele & Miller-Perrin, 1992). Children may be unaware of any difference between the "good" feeling of sexual arousal and the supposed "bad" feeling of sexual abuse (Melton, 1992b). Adding to this confusion is the possibility that, as in the case of intrafamilial abuse, the perpetrator is a known and, often, loved caregiver.

An illustration of some forms of intrafamilial sexual abuse suggests why both children and adults have difficulty understanding childhood sexual abuse. Lawson (1993) described five different types of intrafamilial sexual abuse, including mother–son incest. The first type is *subtle abuse*, which is defined as behavior that is not intended to be sexual or harmful to the child, yet in some way gratifies the perpetrator's sexual needs "at the expense of the child's emotional or developmental needs." This type of abuse does not involve coercion, and it may or may not involve genital contact. Instead, some parents may believe that their child needs special attention, or that their behavior is simply an expression of parent–child love.

The second type of child abuse is *seductive abuse*, defined as sexual stimulation that is inappropriate for the child's age and is motivated by the perpetrator's sexual needs or desires. This type of abuse includes seductive posing or gestures, allowing a child to see nude and/or sexual displays, or verbal arousal.

The third type of abuse is *perverse abuse*, defined as behavior that is intended to sexually humiliate the child. This abuse may include taunting a child about his or her development during puberty, implanting fears about sexual preference in the child, or forcing the child to wear or do things typically associated with the opposite sex.

The fourth type of abuse is *overt sexual abuse*, defined as direct sexual contact between the perpetrator and the child. This abuse includes intercourse, digital penetration, or fondling, and it involves some type of coercion.

The fifth type of abuse is *sadistic sexual abuse*, defined as any sexual behavior that is also intended to physically harm the child. Lawson gave an example of this type of abuse: a boy whose mother sodomized him with a broomstick. He later became a serial killer of women.

Should children be prepared for all the complex, confusing, perverted realities that childhood sexual abuse encompasses? Limited understanding of sexual abuse can leave children unprepared to respond to a perpetrator, yet too much information may deprive them of the safe and secure feelings that they deserve during childhood. Alerting children to the existence of "bad touch" may seem a reasonable compromise between dangerous lack of awareness and brutal overexposure to concepts that alarm even adults.

PREVALENCE OF CHILDHOOD SEXUAL ABUSE

For sexual abuse involving contact between the victim and perpetrator, reported prevalence rates for children under the age of 18 range from 7% to 45% for females and 3% to 5% for males. Other noncontact estimates range from 10% to 62% for females and 3% to 16% for males, depending on the sample population and definition of abuse (i.e., Bolton, Morris, & MacEachron, 1989; Faller, 1989; Finkelhor, 1984; Green, 1993; Russell, 1983; Whitcomb, 1992; Wurtele & Miller-Perrin, 1992). Ratios of girl:boy victims range from 2:1 to 10:1 (e.g., Finkelhor, 1986; Green, 1993).

VULNERABILITY TO CHILDHOOD SEXUAL ABUSE

Melton (1992a) noted that sexually abused children and their families have few features in common. To distinguish between individual traits and environmental forces that contribute to the occurrence of childhood sexual abuse, a distinction is made between vulnerability and risk factors. *Vulnerability* is defined as a characteristic of the child, such as small stature, naivety in social reasoning, or feeling lonely, that increases the likelihood that the child will become a victim. *Risk factors* are defined as situations in the environment that increase the likelihood that the child will be exposed to a perpetrator, such as living in a single-parent home or having a parent who was molested as a child.

Finkelhor (1986) proposed four preconditions necessary for the occurrence of childhood sexual abuse: factors within the perpetrator, the child, the family, and society. Factors within the child include lack of knowledge regarding sexual behavior, hunger for attention, low self-esteem, emotional neediness, and insecurity. Other risk factors include membership in a discordant family, lack of supervision, emotional estrangement from parents, marital conflict involving uneven power distribution between husband and wife, the sexual milieu of the family, isolation of the family, and characteristics of the mother, such as being absent, physically sick, mentally ill, or working outside the home.

Children are particularly vulnerable to incest. Survivors' reports of incest include references to the trickery, deception, coercion, persuasion, and betrayal experienced by children at the hands of a parent or parent figure (Armstrong, 1978; Bass & Davis, 1988; Poston & Lison, 1989). Survivors frequently report feelings of powerlessness in response to a related perpetrator and confusion about whether the sexual activity is some sort of special attention, punishment, or game.

Incest is more likely to occur in households in which the mother was a victim of childhood sexual abuse (Gomes-Schwartz, Horowitz, & Cardarelli, 1990; Goodwin, McCarty, & DiVasto, 1981). Another risk factor is alcohol abuse by the perpetrator (Abel et al., 1987; Finkelhor, 1984). Risk of mother–son incest increases for a boy in a single-mother or lower income household (Banning, 1989). For boys, risk factors associated with being molested outside of the home include: low-income household, divorced parents, neglectful parents, history of runaway, and drug or alcohol use.

Research resulting from the increased reporting of male victims of child sexual abuse has identified potential vulnerabilities and risk factors for boys. For example, Banning (1989) and Vander Mey (1988) determined that, in terms of recognizing and resisting female perpetrators, boys may be vulnerable because early sexual activity for males is viewed as "good experience." In terms of reporting the abuse, boys' vulnerability may be increased due to socialization: to be macho and not show pain, referred to as the "I'm fine" syndrome. Furthermore, boys face negative social consequences for reporting same-sex and incestuous activities, which violate existing taboos.

The occurrence of childhood sexual abuse exposes children's vulnerability in interactions with adults. Melton (1992a) argued for interpretation of children's vulnerability based on knowledge of normal child development. For example, one area of research related to child development focuses on how children acquire trust. *Interpersonal trust* has been defined as "a child's confidence that a person's verbal and nonverbal communications accurately represent, or correspond to, internal states and external events," and includes the child's "sensitivity to lying, deception, and promise violation" (Rotenberg, 1991, pp. 1–2). Bugental, Kopeikin, and Lazowski (1992) determined that children under the age of 7 averted their eyes from the faces of strangers displaying deceptive smiles while continuing to gaze at authentic smiles. By age 10, children ignored deceptive smiles and displayed greater interest in authentic smiles. The authors suggested that the older children understood the false, "polite" smile to be a common, minor social deception, whereas the younger children were confused by a "polite" smile and responded with social avoidance. The authors concluded that the older children's responses reflected "increased understanding of the significance of these two types of smiles'' (p. 75). Girls demonstrated the ability to make this distinction earlier than boys. Abused children at all ages in the Bugental et al. study displayed eye aversion to polite smiles.

Such findings suggest that a child's understanding of social interactions with adults undergoes changes throughout childhood, and that the quality of the adult–child interaction may have a profound effect on a child's chances for normal development. At least two implications of the findings related to social development are relevant to a discussion of childhood sexual abuse. First, the findings suggest that any child may be easy prey for perpetrator deception due to children's undeveloped interpersonal capabilities. Second, abuse, including sexual abuse, may be associated with negative effects for victims, not only in terms of emotional development, but also in the realm of cognitive development, including social reasoning, interpersonal trust, and social inference (Bugental et al., 1992).

AGE FACTORS PERTAINING TO
CHILDHOOD SEXUAL ABUSE

A child's age plays an unclear role in terms of vulnerability to sexual abuse. Childhood sexual abuse has been perpetrated on infants as young as 3.5 months, and has been reported for individuals reaching age 18, at which time they are no longer considered children. The modal age of sexual abuse onset is reportedly around 10 (Peters, Wyatt, & Finkelhor, 1986); the mean age for reporting sexual abuse is also reported to be between 9 and 11 (Gomes-Schwartz et al., 1990). Reports of prevention education efforts suggest that children become less vulnerable to sexual abuse as they grow older (Wurtele & Miller-Perrin, 1992). Daro (1991) stated that perpetrators may target younger children because these children more readily maintain secrecy. Adding to the uncertainty about risks and vulnerability associated with age is the necessary distinction between when abuse *occurs* and when a child *reports* that abuse, or when the abuse is detected. Because many instances of sexual abuse, particularly incest, involve ongoing and escalating activity, the onset of the abuse may precede the reporting or detection of the abuse by many years.

Age may affect childhood sexual abuse in at least two ways. First, increasing age for children is likely to bring decreasing supervision, with older children unsupervised more often than younger children and younger children more likely to be under constant adult care. Thus, younger children may risk being sexually abused by caregivers, such as parents, baby-sitters, and relatives. Older children may be at increased risk for abuse by strangers and acquaintances, such as neighbors, coaches, group leaders, and so on. Second, age is correlated with increased knowledge and awareness of sexual abuse (Wurtele & Miller-Perrin, 1992). Younger children may be abused, but be unaware of the implications of abuse or a need to report:

Developmental variables also contribute to delayed disclosure. Because of their naivete, young children may not know that the activity is wrong or they may lack the verbal ability to report an incident; older children may be too embarrassed to report. Young children's tendency to accommodate to the demands of adults (Summit, 1983) makes it likely that they will participate in the activity and keep the secret. (Wurtele & Miller-Perrin, 1992, p. 16)

Secrecy is a prevalent feature of childhood sexual abuse. Victims do not report their abusers, families do not report the occurrence of incest, and abuse is hidden from extended family, friends, and the community. Only a small percentage of victims may reveal sexual abuse during childhood. For example, Summitt (1983) reported 2% of females experiencing intrafamilial abuse and 6% experiencing extrafamilial abuse. In a previous study by Burkhardt (1986), a majority of children did not report a "stranger" encountered during a safety program, despite previous instructions and a subsequent opportunity to do so.

How is it that children readily and repeatedly report that Sissy took the last piece of cake or that Johnny won't relinquish a toy, even knowing that parents and teachers will harshly rebuff such "tattling," yet they are reluctant to report serious threats to their safety, such as interactions with perpetrators? Fear of repercussions and the promise of gifts may deter children from reporting adults' abuse (Wurtele & Miller-Perrin, 1992). Yet the reasons for children's reluctance to report remain largely unexplained. Perpetrators report their dependence on children's silence (Budin & Johnson, 1989).

In comparison with younger children, greater numbers of older children may report abuse or have abuse detected due to an awareness that reporting is a means to stop the perpetrator. In summary, age and associated factors, such as supervision and social reasoning, are likely to affect children's vulnerability to sexual abuse. There is little certainty, however, regarding who is most vulnerable at what age.

GENDER DIFFERENCES IN CHILDHOOD SEXUAL ABUSE

There is consensus that females are more likely to experience sexual abuse than males. However, there is little agreement as to why or how this is the case. Males may underreport sexual abuse due to socialization factors that dictate that boys be self-reliant, that sexual involvement is normal for boys, that homophobia is masculine, and that being vulnerable is feminine, weak, or socially undesirable (Wurtele & Miller-Perrin, 1992). Still, males' failure to report cannot be used as evidence that the sexual abuse of boys does not occur. Indeed, it has been reported that sex offenders sexually molest young boys at five times the rate of young girls (Abel et al., 1987).

In addition to males underreporting the occurrence of sexual abuse, the subject of boys being victims of child sexual abuse has not been historically examined. The neglect of boy victims may be due, in part, to the issue of childhood sexual abuse first being raised by the women's movement (Banning, 1989). Similarly, the possibility of females being perpetrators of sexual abuse was not seriously considered, with some (see Lawson, 1993) believing females incapable of pedophilia, or sexual attraction to children. However, recent investigations of women as perpetrators and males as victims have appeared (i.e., Banning, 1989; Bolton et al., 1989; Faller, 1989; Harper, 1993; Lawson, 1993).

Gender differences and their role in vulnerability to childhood sexual abuse are important features of a child-generated model. Are girls and boys equally, similarly, and simultaneously vulnerable throughout childhood development? For example, one aspect of children's vulnerability to sexual abuse is their naivety and somewhat automatic adherence to authority (Tutty, 1994). It can neither be assumed nor proved that these tendencies are found only in girls. Similarly, child sexual abuse is associated with certain situational risk factors, such as lower socioeconomic status (SES) and single-parent homes (Vander Mey, 1988). These risk factors are present for both boys and girls. Finally, incarcerated molesters have confessed to sexually abusing both boys and girls, or solely boys (see Freund & Watson, 1992). Measures of sexual arousal confirm molesters' attraction to children, including both boys and girls, which demonstrates perpetrators' preferences for the type of child they abuse (Freund & Watson, 1992). This information makes it conceivable that boys are more likely to be sexually abused and exploited than previously believed.

Increasingly, current research has evaluated gender differences in the occurrence and the effects of childhood sexual abuse (Faller, 1989; Hibbard & Hartman, 1992). Faller's study is commendably thorough, including as much information about each victim and his or her perpetrator as possible, and demonstrating that children of either gender are vulnerable in varying ways. Early reports (Finkelhor, 1984) found boys to be molested at younger ages than girls, suggesting that boys are more vulnerable at earlier ages and girls are more vulnerable at older ages. However, Faller surveyed a clinical sample of 87 male and 226 female children who were victims of sexual abuse, interviewing not only the children but, whenever possible, the perpetrator and a nonoffending parent or parent figure. Faller reported an older age of initiation of abuse for boy victims (6.3 years) compared with the girl victims (5.5 years). Consistent with earlier findings (i.e., Fritz, Stoll, & Wagner, 1981), boys may first become victimized at an older age than girls because boys are more likely than girls to be victimized outside of the home.

Another difference between the girls and boys in Faller's study was that boys abused in the home were more likely than girls to be abused along with other siblings. Of the 13 cases in which boys were sole victims of related perpetrators, 9 of them came from households in which each boy was the only child and, therefore, the main target available to the perpetrator. Boys and girls who were the solitary victims of related perpetrators were the youngest in this study (mean age, 3.6 years). The next youngest group (mean age, 6.2 years) involved boys in families in which several children were abused.

Girls, who are more likely than boys to be sexually abused in the home, may be more accessible to their perpetrators at an earlier age. Boys, who are more likely to be abused away from home than at home, may not become accessible to their potential perpetrators until they are old enough to be out of the house.

In general, all children may share some degree of vulnerability to sexual abuse simply by virtue of being children. Specific risks and vulnerabilities for boys and girls, at different ages throughout childhood and in the company of different types of potential perpetrators, have been suggested, but not reliably determined.

HOW ADULTS VIEW CHILDHOOD SEXUAL ABUSE

In a recent survey of college students, Wellman (1993) determined a difference in views between males and females about childhood sexual abuse. The subjects for this research were students at an urban New England college, whose average age was 20 years. Of the 824 participants, 167 were male and 657 were female; minorities included 4% African American, 9% Hispanic or Latino American, and 1% Asian American. Ninety students declined participation in the study. The subjects were given a 59-item questionnaire, and were instructed to answer each with strongly agree, agree, disagree, or strongly disagree. A sample item is: Most abusers were abused themselves as children. The findings of this survey indicate notable attitude differences about sexual abuse across gender:

1　Males were more likely than females to report feeling ''sexually excited'' when sexual abuse is discussed.

2　Females were more likely than males to report feeling ''frightened'' when sexual abuse is discussed.

3　Males were more likely than females to report believing that childhood sexual abuse victims should not receive therapy for their abuse because it would remind them over and over of the things that happened.

4　Males were more likely than females to report believing that fathers do not approach daughters until the girls reach adolescence.

5　Males were less likely than females to report agreeing that perpetrators should receive long prison sentences.

6　Males were more likely than females to report believing that the children who act ''sexy'' are more likely to be abused or molested.

7　Males were more likely than females to report believing that the recent publicity of childhood sexual abuse is blowing things way out of proportion.

8　Males were less likely than females to report believing that boys are victims of childhood sexual abuse.

9   Males were less likely than females to report believing that incest is sexual abuse.

The findings of the Wellman study raise the possibility that male and female victims of sexual abuse may report and demonstrate different effects from the sexual abuse as a function of a larger, stable set of gender differences in attitudes about sexual abuse.

Understanding childhood sexual abuse means understanding the usual and unusual circumstances under which children may encounter perpetrators, and the possible and necessary responses that children should be prepared to produce to effectively thwart their perpetrators. Given the complexity of social situations that children may encounter, including related perpetrators within the home, deceptive strangers outside the home, and confusing physical and psychological manipulations that children are unable to comprehend, it is little wonder that children may be unprepared to effectively respond to a perpetrator.

PREVENTION OF CHILDHOOD SEXUAL ABUSE

As efforts to prevent childhood sexual abuse rapidly emerged in response to increased reports of victimization, so, too, have questions and concerns about the effectiveness of prevention programs (Finkelhor & Strapko, 1992; Melton, 1992a; Tutty, 1991). Studies of children's responses to abusive adults and situations have offered both promising and challenging findings for concerned caregivers. Simplistic or optimistic adult certainty about the efficacy of instructing children to recognize, resist, and report perpetrators has been tempered with research findings that indicate modest immediate increases in knowledge, diminishing long-term retention of prevention concepts, and unknown changes in actual safety behavior by children after prevention education (Daro, 1991; Finkelhor & Strapko, 1992; Madak & Berg, 1992; Melton, 1992a; Wurtele & Miller-Perrin, 1992). Children have proved more difficult to inoculate against sexual abuse than some adults expected—a finding that undoubtedly does not surprise parents, who are well aware that children do not always do as they are told.

Melton (1992) cautioned against putting the primary responsibility for the prevention of childhood sexual abuse on children. He stated:

> Neither evaluation research nor knowledge about cognitive and social development gives any reason to believe that sexual abuse education programs are effective in preventing abuse. Moreover, on the basis of research on the epidemiology and process of sexual abuse, I have expressed doubt that prevention of sexual abuse is possible, and if it is possible, whether prevention can be achieved without substantial negative side effects. (p. ix)

Although fears that children might be traumatized by prevention education have not been substantiated (Finkelhor & Strapko, 1992; Wurtele & Miller-Perrin,

1992), a more subtle concern may emerge: Perhaps children, due to normal limitations in thinking and reasoning abilities, are "improbable" candidates for protecting themselves from perpetrators, who deliberately exploit children's vulnerability (Finkelhor & Strapko, 1992; Melton, 1992a).

Prevention education research, including long-term and follow-up studies, is likely to continue (Bogat & McGrath, 1993; Hazzard, Webb, Kleemeier, Angert, & Pohl, 1991; Wurtele & Miller-Perrin, 1992). School- and home-based programs for prevention education remain the best established ways to limit new victimization and identify perpetrators. Questions remain, however, regarding how children should be taught to respond to perpetrators.

PREVENTION EDUCATION

Prevention of childhood sexual abuse has become a priority as the negative consequences of victimization have become highlighted. Prevention efforts have primarily targeted children, placing the responsibility (or burden) of prevention on the potential victim (Melton, 1992a; Wurtele & Miller-Perrin, 1992). Both parents and teachers have demonstrated the ability to effectively educate children (even preschoolers) to recognize, resist, and report perpetrators (Wurtele, Kast, & Melzer, 1992), with few reports of negative effects associated with the training. An emphasis on "developmentally appropriate" programs (Wurtele et al., 1992) merely hints at what may be a key feature of successful intervention: knowing what normal boys and girls of various ages are *capable* of understanding in order to prevent childhood sexual abuse.

Prevention education depends on a definition of what constitutes *protection*. Is a child who knows facts about sexual abuse protected from a perpetrator? Is being told what to do if a perpetrator approaches sufficient to guarantee performance of the safety behavior? What concepts can be taught that are compatible not only with what children need to know, but also with what they are *able* to learn?

A survey of teachers by Abrahams, Casey, and Daro, (1992) suggests that teachers may feel unprepared to detect and report child abuse, including sexual abuse, among their students, although there was support for prevention education among those surveyed. Wurtele and Miller-Perrin (1992) indicated:

> We advocate an expansion from a primary focus on classroom-based approaches toward broader and more system-wide reforms. Our thesis is that child-centered approaches can be most effective when augmented by school-, family-, and community-based efforts, each of which should be viewed as contributing toward the prevention of CSA. (p. xii)

Daro (1991) cautioned against reliance on or abandonment of child-focused prevention efforts "in the absence of clear scientific proof regarding the efficacy of these programs," and called on parents and teachers to provide safer environments for children, in addition to preparing the children to protect themselves. Wurtele et al. (1992) discussed children's difficulty with generalization of recognition and resistance skills acquired in personal safety programs, and suggested behavioral remedies to enhance generalization. Although older children have been identified as faster learners of facts about sexual abuse in comparison with younger children (e.g., Finkelhor & Shapko, 1992), the former's advantage has been neither consistent nor long-lived (see Melton, 1992a). No consistent gender differences in prevention education outcomes have been reported (Wurtele et al., 1992).

CHARACTERISTICS OF PERPETRATORS

Little is known for certain about perpetrators of childhood sexual abuse, except that "an overwhelming number are male" (Melton, 1992a, p. 171) and a majority of sex offenders report being victims of childhood sexual abuse (Green, 1993). This suggests that sexual abuse of males is, indeed, more prevalent than believed. That male victims of childhood sexual abuse become sexualized by the experience and are aroused by reenacting abuse in which they are the aggressor may be a disturbing feature of sexual abuse, which is seldom considered outside clinical treatment settings. Some perpetrators report abusing children who remind them of themselves (Budin & Johnson, 1989). Despite assumptions of underlying motivations for perpetrator behavior, it is likely that many perpetrators enjoy sexually abusing children.

Most offenders are related to or acquainted with their victims, thus it is reasonable to assume that, like victims, perpetrators are found in all aspects of society (Melton, 1992). Some offenders repeatedly abuse the same child—a circumstance that is more likely to result in pathology in the victim (i.e., Finkelhor & Browne, 1986; Green, 1993; Terr, 1991). Perpetrators seldom volunteer for treatment (Green, 1993).

In terms of female perpetrators, Faller (1989) found boys 10 times more likely than girls to be sexually abused by their mother or mother figure. However, boys were mostly abused by men, making them more likely than girls to have experienced same-sex abuse (consistent with Fritz et al., 1981). Boys were also more likely than girls to be abused by perpetrators of multiple victims (Faller, 1989; Vander Mey, 1988), and to be abused by professionals outside of the home (Faller, 1989).

Perpetrators, to some extent, are opportunists. As stated by Wurtele and Miller-Perrin (1992), "potential perpetrators must have access to potential victims. Situations in which offenders are alone with children, especially if they are in positions of authority, increase the likelihood of abuse" (p. 34). Perpetrators are assumed to be individuals who fail to inhibit their sexual impulses with children. Finkelhor's (1986) model includes "disinhibition" of the perpetrator as a precondition for the occurrence of sexual abuse. Wurtele and Miller-Perrin (1992) proposed that the "child's initial acceptance of the (sexual) activity or willingness to participate'' may be a ''powerful disinhibitor'' for the perpetrator (p. 32). Thus, a tragic exploitation of children's inability to protect themselves is put in motion: Perpetrators abuse children because children do not stop them and children are unable to stop them because they are children. Thus, children's lack of resistance may be perceived by the perpetrator as permission or entice- ment.

HELPING VICTIMS OF CHILDHOOD SEXUAL ABUSE

For the first time, the *Diagnostic and Statistical Manual of Mental Disorders* (4th ed. [*DSM–IV*]; American Psychiatric Association, 1994) includes sexual abuse within the category *Other Conditions That May Be a Focus of Clinical Attention*. This is in response to public and professional concerns about both perpetrators and victims. Other psychological and behavioral disorders, includ- ing dissociative identity disorder (previously multiple personality disorder), post- traumatic stress disorder, depression, eating disorders, sleep disturbance, sexual dysfunction, and substance abuse, are associated with childhood sexual abuse in both clinical studies and survivor self-reports (e.g., Armstrong, 1978; Green, 1993; Poston & Lison, 1989). Individuals diagnosed with borderline personality disorder often report childhood sexual abuse (American Psychiatric Association, 1994; Green, 1993; Herman & van der Kolk, 1987). However, childhood sexual abuse has not been determined to be a necessary and sufficient cause of any specific psychiatric disorder in *DSM–IV*, despite rigorous speculations and dra- matic claims among treating professionals about the role it is assumed to play in the etiology of psychopathology. The American Psychiatric Association indicates continuing uncertainty regarding the role of childhood trauma in the development of multiple personality disorder, now called dissociative identity disorder (Amer- ican Psychiatric Association, 1994).

Green (1993) suggested eight variables that influence the severity of a vic- tim's symptoms:

1   age and developmental level of the child
2   the child's preexisting personality and resiliency
3   onset, duration, and frequency of abuse
4   degree of coercion and physical trauma
5   the closeness of the relationship between the child and perpetrator
6   the degree of supportiveness of the family's response to disclosure
7   the nature of the institutional response to the abuse, and
8   the availability and quality of therapeutic intervention. (p. 899)

Mannarino, Cohen, and Berman (1994) suggested that the poor psycholog- ical adjustment of some sexually abused children may be a result of both pre- and postabuse factors, as well as ''the trauma of the abusive experience itself'' (p. 63). Even noncoercive sexual abuse may produce psychological disturbance

(Basta & Peterson, 1990). Green (1993) suggested that negative effects of sexual abuse can be minimized or reversed by treatment.

As noted by Green (1993), "there are no specific behavior markers for sexual abuse," and sexual abuse is best considered "an event" rather than a psychiatric disorder (p. 899). For example, Hibbard and Hartman (1992) compared a group of sexually abused children from a child sexual abuse clinic to a group of children being treated for routine well-child care, matched for age, gender, and race. The children were ages 4–8, and 75% were female. The researchers used the Child Behavior Checklist (CBCL) and the Sexual Behavior Scale to assess differences in behaviors, possibly indicating immediate effects of the abuse. The researchers found no significant differences in some of the behavioral symptoms popularly believed to indicate sexual abuse, including: headaches and stomachaches, temper tantrums, thumbsucking, nightmares, enuresis, and withdrawal. Behaviors that were found significantly more often in the sexually abused sample were: demands for attention, attacks on people, excessive sex play, secrecy, sexual problems, strange behavior, sudden mood changes, sleep problems, unhappiness/depression, and excessive worry. The authors caution that, although the results are significant, these behaviors cannot be assumed to indicate abuse because there were numerous reports of the same behaviors in the control sample as well.

In terms of age and gender interactions, the only significant findings involved girl victims between the ages of 4–5 years having high scores on the Schizoid subscale, and boy victims ages 4–5 years having higher scores on the Sex Problems subscale. These findings suggest that males and females may differ in the ways in which they respond to sexual abuse.

Studies involving long-term effects have indicated differences between male and female victims. For example, Friedrich, Urquiza, and Beilke (1986) reported that female victims are more likely than male victims to display internalizing symptoms such as depression or anxiety. Several reviews indicate that male victims of child sexual abuse are more prone than female victims to identify with the perpetrator and later sexually victimize others (i.e., see Banning, 1989; Neilson, 1983; Vander Mey, 1988). Female victims are more likely than male victims to take on a victim role that pervades their later life, with subsequent revictimization at the hands of wife beaters or other molesters (i.e., see Finkelhor, 1984). Furthermore, male victims as adults are more likely than female victims to report the sexually exploiting experience as neutral or even positive (Fritz et al., 1981; Fromuth & Burkhart, 1989; Wellman, 1993).

Gender differences pertaining to sexual abuse may also be present in the professionals who treat the sexually abused. Adams and Betz (1993) assessed gender differences in counselors' attitudes toward incest. The subjects of the study were 67 female and 44 male counselors. Their views about incest and sexual abuse were measured. Regardless of counselor gender, the victims of the abuse were not blamed for their abuse. The researchers found that counselors were less likely than noncounseling samples to blame the victims. Some significant gender differences for counselors were found: Female counselors were more likely than male counselors to be optimistic about the prognosis for the victims to get over their abuse. Male counselors tended to define incest more narrowly than female counselors, and were more likely than female counselors to believe that allegations of incest could be fabricated or just fantasy. These findings suggest that, even among the ranks of the most unbiased and well-educated adults involved with sexual abuse, gender differences may affect attitudes toward victims and perpetrators.

CURRENT CONTROVERSY: REPRESSED VERSUS FALSE MEMORIES

Since Freud, there has been debate regarding the veracity of adult reports of childhood sexual abuse. Adult claims have been considered absolute fact, unconscious fantasy, and undeniable fiction. Recently, in the early 1980s, concerned adults were told by treating professionals and self-styled therapists alike that children were unlikely to fabricate reports of childhood sexual abuse. Concern may have turned to zeal as counselors pursued revelations of childhood sexual abuse in adult clients suffering from a variety of symptoms and disorders (Goldstein, 1992; Wylie, 1993).

In fact, questioning the veracity of childhood sexual abuse reports also became a source of debate. Camps of absolute believers maintained that *all* reports of childhood sexual abuse are unquestionably true; they also took the position that many adults who were victimized have repressed memory of sexual abuse and are in need of retrieving these traumatic memories (Bass & Davis, 1993). In contrast, another camp emerged who worked at debunking the exaggerated reports of adult victims and the therapists who guide the retrieval of repressed memories. Between these two polar positions lie concerned and confused caregivers who do not know who to believe, who to trust, and where to go for a better understanding of real dangers that might exist for today's children.

THE NEED FOR A CHILD-GENERATED MODEL

Children accommodate perpetrators' requests (Summit, 1983). Wurtele and Miller-Perrin (1992) identified guilt, lack of vocabulary, and socialization toward not discussing sex as contributors to children's failure to report perpetrators. Melton (1992a) believed the prevention of sexual abuse is unlikely because children are limited in their self-protection abilities. Despite increased knowledge and awareness about sexual abuse, both on the parts of children and their caregivers, sexual abuse continues and prevention efforts stumble. A fundamental question is: Why?

Finkelhor and Strapko (1992) asserted the need for research studies that "get a large sample of young children to talk candidly about abuse and attempted abuse" involving "intensive investigation-type interviews with children" (pp. 161–162). Indeed, it is necessary to talk with the children; it is equally important to listen to them. Their inability to protect themselves, their reluctance to report perpetrators, and their persistent return to trusting adults may be softly communicating what it means to be a child. Adults, in their urgency to prevent and treat sexual abuse, may not be learning what the children have been teaching. A child-generated model of sexual abuse intervention proposes vehicles for assessing, analyzing, and understanding children's abilities to respond to perpetrators. Before abandoning prevention efforts or debating the retrieval of repressed memories, it may be helpful to establish the parameters of childhood capabilities. Based on knowledge of developmental contributions to childhood sexual abuse, those adults trying to prevent and treat childhood sexual abuse will be prepared to meet the children where they are.

SUMMARY

Chapter 1 provided an overview of topics related to childhood sexual abuse, particularly those that relate to children's ability to understand sexual abuse. Childhood vulnerability to perpetrators was introduced, and the controversy regarding how and why prevention programs are not as effective as hoped for was explored. Factors related to vulnerability, including age and gender differences, suggested that additional study of how normal children think and act in response to adults, including perpetrators, is needed. A rationale for a child-generated model of sexual abuse intervention was presented: to discover how well prepared children are in terms of understanding sexual abuse and how well prepared they can become.

Chapter 2

Correlates of
Child Sexual Abuse

The search for greater understanding of how and why child sexual abuse occurs leads to an examination of characteristics of children themselves. The aim is to identify factors that contribute to children's vulnerability. *Vulnerability* is defined as physical and/or psychological characteristics of children associated with reducing their safety or protection. The definition excludes risk factors, which are situations and circumstances that increase the likelihood of abuse (e.g., presence of a stepfather in the home). Rather, vulnerability refers to those features, specific to children, that may make them targets for sexually abusive advances.

Theories of childhood vulnerability to sexual abuse have included intrapsychic, biological, social, and familial contributions. Theories, mostly untested, regarding victim variables have flourished, and positions on the victim's possible role in victimization cover the gamut. The child has been portrayed as everyone from instigator and solicitor of the adult perpetrator, to the hapless target of men's misguided rage at women (Rush, 1980). In the following sections, theories of child sexual abuse are reviewed.

THEORIES DERIVED FROM THE
PSYCHOANALYTIC TRADITION

Psychosexual stages of development have been discussed as the groundwork laid by psychoanalytic theory in support of labeling children as the instigators of sexual abuse (Finkelhor, 1979; Furniss, 1991; Rush, 1980). At the core of the conflict during the phallic stage of psychosexual development is a child's fantasy of sexually possessing the opposite sex parent. Freud's work, including the treatment of hysterical adult females in a Victorian era, revealed patient confessions of childhood sexual experiences with trusted adults, relatives, and even fathers. In 1896, Freud proposed his seduction theory, which maintained that these incidents of childhood sexual experiences at the hands of significant adults were instrumental in the development of subsequent psychoneuroses (Rush, 1980). However, Freud later reversed his positions on childhood sexuality, for reasons that remain unclear (Masson, 1984), and maintained that the reported sexual incidents were products of female fantasies fueled by id impulses residing within the child rather than the adult. These fantasies, rich grist for the analyst's mill, did not betray transgressing adult men, but, rather, the deeply repressed female desire for the forbidden. If, in fact, sexual activity did occur between a girl and an adult male, the likely cause would be the seductiveness of the child (Deutsch, 1973; Rush, 1980). Unresolved conflicts of an oedipal nature were considered the underlying dynamic of the sexually provocative child (Finkelhor, 1986; Masson, 1984; Rush, 1980).

FAMILY SYSTEMS THEORY

Family systems theory has offered a view of familial conditions, including the child's role in the family, that may lead to and maintain sexual activity between children and adult family members. This theory distributes responsibility for incest across members of the family, and explores the ways in which individuals may knowingly or unknowingly set up incestuous expression (Strauss, 1973; Trepper & Barrett, 1986). Incest may serve to deflect or diffuse marital conflict, and, as such, the child victim may be participating in incest to "save" the family (Giaretto, 1976; Larson & Maddock, 1986). The child, as part of the family system, necessarily shares responsibility for the sexual expression. The child may willingly participate in incest because of the benefits it has for him or her (usually her). For example, a daughter may be reluctant to give up her "privileged status" as daddy's favorite (Larson & Maddock, 1986). In family systems theory, the victim's vulnerability stems from membership in a dysfunctional family. Finkelhor (1986) and Conte (1986) noted that the family systems conceptualization of childhood sexual abuse does not provide an explanation of abuse perpetrated by nonfamily members, yet nonfamilial abuse appears to be the most common type (Finkelhor, 1979; Kinsey, Pomeroy, Martin, & Gebhard, 1953; Russell, 1984).

SOCIOCULTURAL THEORIES

Social, political, and cultural theories, many proposed by feminists, view men's sexual exploitation of children as an extension of men's sexual exploitation of women (Brownmiller, 1975; Rush, 1980). Men are seen as inclined to indulge their sexual and aggressive appetites as they choose, with a male-dominated society permitting its cohorts to exploit without fear of serious retribution. Young, small, and attractive targets are desired, and conquest is reasonably assured. The sexual abuse of children is a symptom of the power inequities between men and women; sexual abuse is likely to occur in a society in which women and children are seen as males' property (Brownmiller, 1975; Herman & Hirschman, 1977, 1981). This view of child vulnerability considers the individual attributes of any particular child of minimal relevance. The child is seen as a symbol of the abstract societal battle of the sexes. This literature strongly refutes the notion of the child victim bearing any responsibility for his or her participation in sexual activity with an adult, and openly defies the Freudian notion of the female child as co-perpetrator or seductress (Bass & Davis, 1988; Rush, 1980).

EDUCATIONAL DEFICITS

Children's lack of information and knowledge about sex and, specifically, sexual abuse are assumed sources of childhood vulnerability (Finkelhor, 1986). Children are seen as socially groomed for conformity and passivity, and thus they do not know when or how to resist and report inappropriate actions or requests by adults (Kraizer, 1985; Lenett, 1985; Newman, 1985). Prevention efforts have focused on remediating educational deficits.

An assessment of children's conceptions about sexual abuse was undertaken by Wurtele and Miller (1987). Forty-eight children, 20 ages 5–7 and 28 ages 10–12, were read a vignette describing sexual abuse. They were then asked to hypothesize about the nature of sexual abuse in general, the attributes of the victim and the perpetrator, and the consequences of the abuse for both. The two age groups differed in all assessed aspects of understanding sexual abuse. The older children were more aware of and accurate in their knowledge of what constitutes sexual abuse and characteristics of victims and perpetrators. Older subjects were also more likely to make psychological attributions regarding the perpetrator's motivations and the negative consequences to the victim. Interestingly, many older subjects believed the perpetrator would be helped by psychological treatment rather than criminal prosecution. Subject recommendations for dealing with a perpetrator included saying "no," getting away, and reporting the perpetrator to an authority figure. Nineteen percent of all subjects were unable to offer any suggestions for resisting or reporting a perpetrator. A majority of both age groups (70% of the younger subjects, 89% of the older ones) were able to provide suggestions for resistance rated as "constructive." In general, Wurtele and Miller's study suggests that children's knowledge about sexual abuse increases with age.

Children vary in their knowledge about sexual abuse, leading to the conclusion, perhaps, that eliminating educational deficits can eliminate vulnerability.

For example, popular books decree a "knowledge is power" maxim, and address ignorance by providing detailed information about the dangers of strangers and the discomfort of "bad touch" (Dayee, 1982; Kraizer, 1985; Lenett, 1985; Newman, 1985). Prevention materials and programs provide parents and even the youngest children with information and training about assertiveness techniques in an attempt to fulfill Dayee's (1982) promise that "informed children are safer children." The efficacy of prevention efforts is discussed in chapter 5.

BIOLOGICAL AND PSYCHOLOGICAL CONTRIBUTIONS TO VULNERABILITY

A variety of other childhood attributes have led theorists to propose physical and biological contributions to childhood vulnerability. Obvious physical features, such as small stature and limited strength for resistance, have been mentioned (Finkelhor, 1979). Physically attractive children have been identified as more likely targets for sexual advances by adults, as have children who enter into puberty at an early age (Finkelhor, 1979; Gentry, 1978). However, physically and mentally deficient children have also been identified as at risk (Armstrong, 1978). With the exception of the group of child abusers known as pedophiles, who experience intense sexual arousal primarily or solely with children, there is lack of agreement regarding why adult perpetrators, many of whom have adult sexual partners, choose children for sexual activity (Langevin, Day, Handy, & Russon, 1985).

Personality features associated with or attributed to victims of sexual abuse and incest include passivity (Burton, 1968; Finkelhor, 1979; Trepper & Barrett, 1986), trust (Finkelhor, 1986), dependence and sociopathy (Trepper & Barrett, 1986), need for attention and affection (Burton, 1968; Gentry, 1978), low self-esteem (Frude, 1982; Justice & Justice, 1979), and fear of abandonment (Askwith, 1982; Finkelhor, 1979; Tierney & Corwin, 1983). A commonly expressed belief of victims is that they were somehow to blame for the abuse (Armstrong, 1978; Bass & Davis, 1988; Finkelhor, Gelles, Hotaling, & Straus, 1983). These traits, however, have not been systematically researched as to their part in victimization. Their role in causing abuse has not been established, and one might well argue that such traits are the result, rather than the cause, of victimization.

COGNITIVE VULNERABILITY

An explanation of children's cognitive developmental vulnerability to sexual abuse by adults is notable by its absence. Children are not only physically unsuited to resist adult advances, but their reasoning and judgment capabilities may be inadequate to meet the social demand of responding to an adult's abusive use of authority. It is also possible that even when a child knows that a response is needed, he or she may be unable to choose or execute an effective response.

Research in cognitive development, particularly in the realm of social cognition, has made strides in identifying the qualitative and quantitative differences between childhood reasoning abilities and adult logic.

A DEVELOPMENTAL PERSPECTIVE

A developmental perspective studies changes over a period of growth. Child development looks at the rapid changes and acquisitions of new capabilities that typify human beings during their early years. Reviewing childhood development to unravel some of the puzzling aspects of vulnerability to sexual abuse serves two major purposes. First, developmental research methods solicit systematic input from the individuals being studied; the children express their points of view and describe events in their own words. Children's ideas and beliefs about sexual abuse need to be heard, examined, and understood if adults are to succeed in changing children's vulnerability to sexual abuse. Minimally, the children should be heard, in their own voices, to further adult understanding. Optimally, solutions to children's vulnerability may be found by tapping and building on their existing levels of reasoning.

Second, a developmental study of any social problem offers to professionals and parents a firm grasp of what children can and cannot be expected to do, especially at certain ages. Developmental studies place their emphasis on the collection of information from typical children, so that such data may serve as a baseline against which other children's responses can be compared. Deviations from the norm, some possibly pathological, can be more readily identified if parameters for what is typical have been established. In the area of childhood sexual abuse, it may be premature to label an incest victim as needy, seductive, precocious, or disturbed if, in fact, one discovers that many children would think, act, or respond to the same situation in a similar manner.

An investigation of children's reasoning requires the researcher and reader to delve into a literature that tells the adult world what it is to think as a child. It requires a fondness for listening to children with a patient ear and resisting the temptation to "teach" away their "faulty" logic. New levels of understanding children's vulnerability are a product of exploring and appreciating that which the children see. Asking children to problem solve in the confusing realm of human sexuality brings with it even greater demands for quiet, reassuring, and nonjudgmental listening on the part of the audience.

COGNITIVE DEVELOPMENT

Research into cognitive development charts the course of how human beings develop an understanding of their world, themselves, and each other. Perhaps there is no simple way to define *cognitive development*. It is the growth, accumulation, and expansion of uniquely human mental abilities, described by Flavell (1985) as "knowledge, consciousness, intelligence, thinking, imagining, creating, generating plans and strategies, reasoning, inferring, problem-solving, conceptualizing, classifying and relating, symbolizing, and perhaps fantasizing and dreaming'' (p. 2).

The growth, accumulation, and expansion of cognitive abilities occur throughout childhood. Developmental researchers are often posed two general types of questions: What? and When? At what age will Jane be able to remember her phone number? When will Johnny understand that the stove is hot? Should children be taught counting in first grade, or can instruction begin in preschool? Selman (1980) acknowledged that a desirable goal of cognitive developmental research would be the designation of age ranges for the emergence of reasoning stages. Questions regarding What? and When? have been addressed, but not always with the definitive age markers parents and teachers might like.

The study of cognitive development in children reveals two "truths." First, cognitive abilities become more sophisticated and complex with increasing age. Piaget and Kohlberg (cited in Gelman & Baillargeon, 1983) as well as others (e.g., Flavell, 1985; Selman, 1980) have established a positive correlation between chronological age and improved cognitive capacity and efficiency. For example, memory capacity, problem-solving abilities, social and moral reasoning, and the use of logic have all been found to improve as children grow older. However, a second "truth" also consistently appears. Normal age ranges for the development of cognitive capabilities are extremely broad, often spanning intervals of 5–8 years. Improvement is not steadily forward moving; there may be starts, stops, and slips as abilities emerge. Therefore, although one may claim with great certainty that little Patsy will become more cognitively capable as she grows older, one is unable to predict with great accuracy the precise age at which a particular ability will emerge.

STAGE THEORY

Piaget (1970) conceptualized cognitive development as a series of stages through which a child passes. These stages are seen as standard, invariant in sequences, and characterized by changes in the quality of how the child thinks, knows, and understands not only the world, but him- or herself. The developmental process itself is seen as involving a gradual "leg-over-leg" (Flavell, 1985) progression, in which new sensory input is compared to existing knowledge (schema) for detection of similarities (assimilation). At the same time, the existing knowledge is expanded to incorporate any novelties of the new input (accommodation).

For example, if a child visits the zoo for the first time and happens upon a zebra, he or she may assimilate the animal to his or her existing scheme for four-legged, horse-type creatures, but he or she must expand his or her existing knowledge to accommodate the stripes. Should the child encounter something that is to him or her imperceptibly different from existing knowledge (e.g., a mule), he or she may end up forgetting or including it in the horse category without qualification because he or she is unable to attend to such minute differences in a meaningful way. Thus, input that is not recognized as different in comparison to existing knowledge is likely to be ignored or denied (Darley, Glucksberg, Kamin, & Kinchla, 1981).

PIAGETIAN STAGES

Piagetian stage theory (Piaget, 1970) involves four stages of cognitive development. The *sensorimotor* stage encompasses roughly the first 24 months of life, and is characterized by a progression from reflexive imitation to symbolic thinking (Flavell, 1985). The *preoperational* stage spans from about age 2 to age 7, and is characterized by reasoning that is contradictory, intuitive rather than logical, and reliant on idiosyncratic rather than consensual data. For the child in this stage, the world is as it appears. For example, the neighbor boy wearing a werewolf mask for Halloween becomes a werewolf while wearing the mask in the eyes of a preoperational child. Similarly, a person who acts friendly or smiles happily is, necessarily, a nice person (DeVries, 1969; Flavell, 1985).

From approximately 7–11 years of age, children are in the *concrete operational* stage of reasoning. They demonstrate an ability to use logical thought processes pertaining to concrete objects. *Formal operational* thinking, usually beginning after the age of 11, involves the ability to reason about abstract and hypothetical concepts in a logical manner (Hoffman, Paris, Hall, & Schell, 1988).

In a formulation of moral development, Kohlberg (1976) identified stages in reasoning about moral rather than physical problems. His stages parallel those of Piaget and include improvement, expansion, and increasing complexity in reasoning abilities. In general, stage theory envisions marked, steplike growth in cognitive functioning that, although influenced by environmental factors and experience, unfolds according to a maturational schedule.

INFORMATION-PROCESSING MODEL OF COGNITIVE DEVELOPMENT

An information-processing model of cognitive development represents cognitive abilities as analogous to a computer's functions and capacities. Environmental input is like bits of information in need of processing by the system. The human cognitive system is believed to have limits to how much and how well it can process input or manipulate symbols (Siegler, 1983; Sternberg & Powell, 1983). Cognitive performance would necessarily depend on the amount of information the system could handle at any given point in time and the efficiency of the existing memory banks and programs. Processing tasks (i.e., recognizing, understanding, problem solving), which demand more resources than the system possesses, are viewed as "overloading" that system, resulting in a failure to accomplish the task. Increased processing capacity is developed as a function of experience and neurological maturation.

MODELS OF COGNITIVE DEVELOPMENT COMPARED

Differences between the information-processing model of cognitive development and the traditional Piagetian view include the following. First, the former holds that the improvement of reasoning abilities is not accomplished in abrupt, forward leaps envisioned by stage theory. Second, proponents of information processing do not consider the differences between how adults and children gain knowledge, or achieve expertise, as fundamentally different or particularly great (i.e., Flavell, 1985; Nisbett & Ross, 1980; Siegler, 1983). In general, both the Piagetian and information-processing models of cognitive development provide for changes in children's cognitive abilities through assimilation and accommodation along some time line, with environmental interaction seen as instrumental to the process.

Both models acknowledge the existence of an interesting and persistent type of "cognitive shortcoming"—egocentrism (Flavell, 1985). *Egocentrism* is the human tendency to readily access one's own point of view without equal facility in recognizing someone else's point of view. Piaget suggested that egocentric thinking was an early childhood phenomenon, whereas Flavell (1985) and others (e.g., Elkind, 1967; Tversky & Kahneman, 1973) argued that a tendency toward egocentric thinking is part of the human condition.

Much of the work in the area of cognitive development reflects how human beings come to know and understand their physical world. In addition to knowledge of inanimate objects, people accumulate knowledge and develop understanding about themselves and each other. This world of knowledge about uniquely human interactions is the realm of social cognition.

SOCIAL COGNITION

The development of social cognition involves the process by which children come to know how others think and feel (Shantz, 1975). Social cognition is complex, involving more than the mere use of reasoning capabilities to trying to figure out people rather than objects (Selman, 1980). For example, a child may discover that hugging a pillow offers comfort. However, the same child may discover that hugging a person does not guarantee comfort, especially if the person being hugged is an irritated older sister or an impatient father trying to rush to work. People, unlike objects, have their own internal states that may be revealed, but can be concealed.

Social cognition includes not only knowledge of others but also of the self (Butterworth & Light, 1982). Flavell (1985), in agreement with Butterworth, viewed increasing self-awareness as an integral part of social cognition. Finally, the development of social cognition involves not only knowing others, not only knowing self, but also knowing self and others in relationship to each other.

By exploring the features of how children normally understand and respond to adults, there is, perhaps, an opportunity to determine how cognitive vulnerability may affect children's ability to know, understand, and react to a perpetrator. The study of social cognition has been varied in its theories and methods. Application of these methods to the realm of sexually abusive interactions extends beyond the usual field of study into an arena of deviant social encounters.

CONDITIONS OF SOCIAL COGNITION

Flavell (1985) offered a generic formulation of preconditions for social thinking: existence, need, and inference. *Existence* is knowing that a social world exists. To think about something, one must know that it is there to think about. *Need* refers to the motivation to figure out the meaning of actions that occur in this social sphere. Finally, *inference* is the ability to successfully accomplish social thinking or to formulate a social response.

Sexual abuse involves a child having an inappropriate social interaction with an adult or a significantly older child. A Piagetian analysis of the tasks involved in such a social encounter involves several steps (Piaget, 1970). First, the child is called on to assimilate the interaction, indexing similarities between this abusive and sexually toned encounter and previous social encounters with adults. Additionally, the child must accommodate the unique features of an abusive situation. The interaction lends itself not only to the child's social cognitive examination of another person (i.e., What do I know and understand about this adult?), but also an examination of self (i.e., What do I know and understand about myself in this interaction?). Finally, the child may reflect on the social meaning of the interaction, not only at the time of the encounter, but also retrospectively.

CHILD–ADULT SOCIAL INTERACTIONS

Flavell (1985) indicated that children try to "read" people and use "inferential skills that make these readings meaningful and useful" (p. 121). Drawing on a benign interaction, such as being told to pick up toys, a pattern of social cognitive activity can be proposed. First, a child discovers that an adult directive carries an expectation of compliance (existence). Through cognitive maturation and experience, a child learns that the event of being directed by an adult signals the existence of a social dilemma of sorts. Next, the child develops a motivation to identify the nature of the social demand (need). Again, through maturation and experience, it is usual that a child determines whether the adult issuing the directive warrants a response. The young child may know that the directive needs a response and, therefore, collapses in a fit of tantrum or readily throws toys in the basket in hopes of hurrying to the snack table. The older child may recognize the social need to respond and state "Okay, later." Each child attempts to determine what, if any, response is desirable or needed, and which responses are likely to be effective (inference). One suspects that even young children develop some facility in the social game of child–adult interactions.

The conditions for social cognition can be imposed on the child–perpetrator interaction. Here the child is confronted with a social interaction that includes some type of sexual implication. The child's awareness of the existence of this type of social interaction may range from virtually no knowledge at all, through superficial awareness, to complete knowledge. Providing there is some degree of awareness, the child's motivation to think about a sexually toned interaction with an adult may range from no motivation at all to intense motivation and desire to understand. The levels of inference range from no skill at processing what may be very unusual social information, to emerging cognitive skill that is inadequate or inaccurate, to outright competence that reflects an understanding of a perpetrator's sexual demands or expectations.

Do children recognize the social demand placed on them in a sexually abusive interaction with an adult perpetrator? What is the child's capacity for crafting a response to such a demand? Insofar as a child is unable to demonstrate optimal functioning in any of the three conditions, that child can be seen as "vulnerable" to sexual abuse. Further, even if a child realizes the existence of the sexually toned social information, is motivated to figure out its meaning, and is able to think of a social response, the facility and competency with which the response is enacted may be ineffective in thwarting a perpetrator. It is at the elementary level of knowing, understanding, and creating a social response to an adult that children may possess "developmental" vulnerability.

ORGANIZING PRINCIPLES IN SOCIAL COGNITION

At first consideration, one might concede that children are necessarily limited in their knowledge of sexually inappropriate interactions with adults. Such encounters are both socially deviant and atypical. Therefore, it is assumed (and hoped) that few children acquire direct experience in order to develop knowledge and understanding of perpetrators. Is it logical, then, to conclude that all children who have not been approached by a perpetrator lack the necessary experience to develop social competencies to thwart a sexually abusive action?

The answer seems to be no. Many children may possess the needed competencies to deter a perpetrator, but may not have encountered a social situation in which these skills were needed. How would these skills be developed? Damon (1977) argued against social knowledge being viewed as a mere collection of unrelated social lessons learned by a child over time. Rather, he maintained that social knowledge reflects the development and application of organizing principles that guide the child's interactions with others.

Organizing principles change as the child grows. Still, even young children use organizing principles to govern their social interactions, although their rules may seem primitive and simplistic to the adult observer. One task of a developmental researcher is to identify the principles used by children at various ages to determine the nature and course of children's emerging social competencies. These principles are characterized by *stability, consistency of use,* and *spontaneity.*

Organizing principles are stable in that they emanate from the child's own reasoning about a social event and are not mere products of what the child has been told to think about the event. For example, a young child's social reasoning "I like Uncle Bob because he gives me candy" may be based on an organizing principle that reserves "liking" for those people who give the child gifts. Stability is demonstrated as the child continues to like Uncle Bob even in the face of others telling him that Uncle Bob is mean or bad. The child continues to like Bob because the child has an ongoing, or stable, reason for liking him—Uncle Bob gives the child gifts.

Organizing principles are also consistently used across social events. For the previous example, the child demonstrates consistency of use as he or she extends "liking" to everyone, and anyone, who gives him or her a gift. The child may explain that he or she likes Sammy because Sammy gave him or her a birthday present.

Finally, organizing principles are characterized by spontaneity in that the child, without prompting or being told to do so, employs the principle as a means to choose a social response. The child uses his or her organizing principle "I like people who give me presents" to navigate numerous social situations. Logically then, the child asks people "Did you bring me a present?" and bestows smiles and "liking" on strangers who come bearing gifts. As many parents realize, despite frequent parental warnings about selfishness, greed, rudeness, and danger, the young child is apt to spontaneously apply his or her organizing principle as he or she sees fit, without concern for manners or safety. Also, as most parents know, a child's own reasons for his or her behavior are more dearly held than any supplied by the parent, who is trying to influence and guide that behavior.

AUTHORITY REASONING

One aspect of social cognition that is relevant to the study of children's vulnerability to sexual abuse involves children's social perceptions and understanding of adults. Adults and children are not peers in the social arena, and children quickly learn that authority is a component in their interactions with adults (Youniss, 1980). Damon (1977), although not specifically addressing abuses by adults, asserted that children do not merely learn rules to govern their responses to authority, but also develop rationales for obedience.

In his studies of children's views of authority, Damon delineated three major levels of childhood reasoning about authority, established that children use the concept of *authority* as an organizing principle in responding to adults, and demonstrated that older children tend to use more advanced reasoning levels than younger children. His cross-sectional and longitudinal studies serve to outline the general course of social cognitive development while taking note of interesting detours that development makes along the way.

Bogat and McGrath (1993) employed Damon's framework for understanding how children view authority in their study of preschoolers' responses to abusive and benign social situations with adults. They concluded that prevention education increased the children's social reasoning about perpetrators by informing children that perpetrators lack a satisfactory reason for abusing children. The authors suggest that research of authority and sexual abuse would be strengthened by the use of stimulus stories, similar to Damon's, that involve abusive events. The Burkhardt study, explained in the following sections, does exactly that.

LEVELS OF REASONING ABOUT ADULT AUTHORITY

Three major levels of authority reasoning, each with two sublevels, reported by Damon (1977) and summarized by Bogat and McGrath (1993) suggest what type of social reasoning is normal and typical for children. Authority reasoning has been found to increase with chronological age. No differences in reasoning capabilities between boys and girls have been noted. Two concepts related to children's views on authority include the *legitimacy* of the authority figure and the *rationale* for obedience. *Legitimacy* has been defined as "the justification for social power" (Damon, 1977, p. 172), and has to do with an authority figure's "right" to command. *Rationale for obedience* is the "justification for obedience, as well as disobedience" (Damon, 1977, p. 173), and focuses on reasons for obeying and consequences of not obeying. The following sections summarize the general characteristics of authority reasoning.

Level 0-A

Level 0-A reasoning about authority is characterized by the child confusing his or her own desires with the authority figure's commands. At Level 0-A, children lack both a rationale for obedience and an understanding of the legitimacy of authority. Obedience and legitimacy are equated with desire (i.e., "I obey because I want to" and "I listen to Mommy and Daddy because I like to"). Level 0-A reasoning was found in children at age 4, but was typically absent in children beyond this age.

A sexually abusive encounter with an adult perpetrator at this tender age might render a child victim convinced of his or her own desire for the event. Such conviction, "I touched Mr. X. when he told me to because I wanted to," may have less to do with the realization of Oedipal urges and more to do with the young child's egocentric perspective, or his or her inability to attribute any event to anything other than his or her own desire, wishes, or control.

Level 0-B

Level 0-B reasoning, demonstrated in children ages 4–6, shares elements of Level 0-A. Egocentrism, or the child's tendency to focus solely on self, is a central feature of reasoning at this level. At Level 0-A, there is a merging between what self and other wants. At Level 0-B, the opposite occurs. The child sees authority for what it often is: an obstacle to having what the self really wants.

At Level 0-B, obeying authority or avoiding authority are equally meritorious. Authority is legitimized by superficial, concrete, and physical attributes: "I obey Mommy and Daddy because they are grown-ups (or tall, or live at my house)." Level 0-B authority is perceived as authority insofar as it requires the child to do something he or she does not want to do. Anyone who has ever witnessed a normal 5-year-old turn from a sweet, well-mannered playmate into an oppositional, tantrum-threatening hellion simply because he or she has been told that it is time for his or her friend to go home has anecdotal evidence that obedience at this age does not stem from valuing authority. For the Level 0-B reasoner, obedience is good only if it nets the child rewards or helps avoid negative consequences.

At Level 0-B, a child would have limited ability to rationally navigate a sexually abusive encounter with a perpetrator. All directives are experienced as impinging on the child's freedom, and the child is unable to conceive of any benefits associated with delaying his or her own wishes. If all requests by authority are perceived as threats to the child's independence, then a sexually abusive advance may be perceived as no more, or less, outrageous than a directive to pick up one's toys or put on a clean shirt.

The Level 0-B reasoner uses a rationale for obedience that does not distinguish between fair and unfair commands: One obeys when one must and one disobeys when one can. A sexually abusive encounter may well be managed in the same fashion: Submit if one must and flee if one can. Although the fleeing may actually offer children this age some protection from perpetrators, it is also likely that the Level 0-B reasoner may be particularly vulnerable to promises of candy, toys, or a ride to an amusement park because such promises may reflect children's own egocentric wishes or fantasies.

Level 1-A

Authority Level 1-A marks a substantial change in the child's view of authority. Authority figures are now invested with an inherent right-to-govern and to be obeyed. Authority figures are deserving of respect, rather than fear, because they possess "legitimizing" attributes, such as physical or social power. The child obeys his or her parents because they are Mommy and Daddy. There is a belief in the overall, although unspecific, superiority and omniscience of authority.

Obedience becomes valued for its righteousness. Authority figures can be neither deceived nor escaped.

Level 1-A reasoning, found in children as young as ages 4-7, may usher in a particular element of vulnerability. Whereas Level 0 allowed children to disobey when, and if, they wanted to and could, Level 1 children are compelled to obey by newfound constraint on disobedience: morality. Disobedience is allowed only in cases in which authority orders a clearly wrong or harmful act, such as stealing or doing something dangerous. Little is known about whether a child views a sexually abusive act as potentially harmful or wrong. If a child is unsure of the potential harm of a directive, he or she may feel compelled to obey simply because authority figures deserve to be obeyed. Attempts to escape or defy authority may be seen as futile by the Level 1-A child, who believes authority to be all-knowing and all-powerful.

Level 1-B

Level 1-B involves the child's continued belief that he or she occupies a deservedly subordinate position compared with an authority figure. However, there is a budding notion of reciprocity in the authority relationship: One gives obedience to a superior who possesses particular attributes that serve the best interest of the subordinate. A child obeys his or her parents because they have special knowledge about what is best for the child. Authority figures deserve obedience because of past, present, or future favors. The Level 1-B reasoner is capable of voluntarily submitting to the will of authority in the belief that such submission is a means of actually helping "self." Level 1-B reasoning was found in children ranging from ages 6 to 9 years.

In terms of vulnerability to sexual abuse, the Level 1-B child may conclude that a sexually abusive encounter with an adult is not harmful, but rather may be helpful, good, or in the child's best interests. A Level 1-B child believes his or her superiors know best, and that by allowing him- or herself to be ruled by such superiors, the children is helped. A perpetrator may be viewed by the child as more knowledgeable in the realm of sexual or affectionate exchanges, and the child may see the perpetrator's interest as assistance in learning about sex—a rather curious aspect of social life. One anecdotal report made to the author by a 9-year-old girl revealed the child's speculation that a father might want to do "bad touch stuff" with his daughter so that he could teach her about sex. The girl expressed her belief that a father might be the appropriate person to teach a child about sex because "parents are the ones who teach their kids about almost everything, except school stuff."

Level 2-A

At Level 2-A, ages 8–9, authority is viewed by the child as a relationship between equals. Authority figures are leaders or experts in specific areas, but not superior persons in and of themselves. "Good authority" figures are concerned about the welfare as well as the rights and feelings of the subordinate. Finally, authority figures are believed to be fallible. Obedience is totally voluntary at Level 2-A, and without obligation: Subordinates obey because a command is a good one, given for a good reason. Unfair or unwise commands need not be obeyed. One may choose to obey a bad command for the purpose of avoiding negative consequences, but doing so is seen as strictly pragmatic and not based on a moral obligation to follow the commands of the authority figure. Cooperative obedience is viewed as superior.

Level 2-B

By age 9, Level 2-B reasoning may be in evidence. As in Level 2-A, authority relations are seen as reciprocal rather than authoritarian. Authority at Level 2-B is seen as situation-specific and temporary, established and removed by consensus. Even the long-standing authority roles—parent and teacher—are considered legitimate only under appropriate conditions and only by agreement of the governed. A legitimizing trait in one area does not entitle the authority to dictate in other areas. Mom and Dad, experts in doing laundry, are not entitled to select the child's school clothing, a domain in which the child is the best authority. As in Level 2-A, obedience is in the service of avoiding chaos and is seen as a voluntary contribution to a cooperative effort. Further, the authority role is reversible, with the child entitled to be the authority figure in his or her own areas of expertise. For example, a Level 2-B reasoner may conclude, "I am entitled to boss my parents around at my school because I know more about this place than they do."

In some regards, children with Level 2 reasoning should demonstrate reduction in vulnerability to sexual abuse because they do not believe they must comply with all directives given by authority figures. However, a Level 2 child is prepared to defer to an authority figure who demonstrates a specific expertise that is unknown to the child. If a perpetrator is perceived as a "sex" or affection expert, and the child is interested in gaining expertise in these areas, a Level 2 child may comply with a perpetrator's directives. Also, a perpetrator who deceives a child into believing that it is the child who can teach the perpetrator might also entice a child into acting as the "authority" in the exploration of sexual activity. Finally, at Level 2, children continue to comply, albeit grudgingly, with authority figures for the sole purpose of avoiding conflict. A child might go along with a sexual advance, despite feeling resentment or distress, just to avoid making trouble, as when a child this age complies with cleaning his or her room simply to avoid a fight.

UNDERSTANDING AUTHORITY

Children's capacity to understand authority follows a progression from egocentric explanations and reliance on external physical attributes to awareness that power resides in both situational factors and expertise. There emerges a realization that authority figures have spheres of influence, domains of authority, and limits to their power. Finally, rule by consensus evolves as a requirement for the legitimacy of authority.

Children can and do offer explanations of legitimacy and obedience. They attempt to sort out which people should be obeyed, when they should be obeyed, and why they should be obeyed. As children determine the boundaries of an authority figure's domain, it is reasonable to assume that these inexperienced "reasoners" may demonstrate errors in judgment regarding the legitimacy of authority and the rationale for obedience. Such errors may constitute another aspect of cognitive vulnerability to sexual abuse. For example, a child gives a parent's demands considerable legitimacy because the parent occupies a readily identified position of authority. Under what circumstances would and could the child justify disobeying the parent? How wrong must a directive be before a child truly believes in his or her right to disobey?

It can be predicted that parental legitimacy is the strongest of any adult authority figure. The literature on incest suggests that sexually abusive advances from fathers and male relatives are particularly difficult for child victims to understand, resist, or report (e.g., Armstrong, 1978; Finkelhor, 1979; Rush, 1980). Other authority figures may be vested with varying degrees of legitimacy.

When the man down the street tells a child to stay off the grass, does the child feel the same mandate to comply as when the child's teacher tells him or her to turn in homework? It is easy to imagine a child's confusion regarding how to respond to an inappropriate directive (e.g., "Come here and rub my back") if it is issued by an adult who is vested with legitimate authority, such as a teacher, coach, clergyman, or scout leader. The "wrongness" of the directive may be unclear to a child while the legitimacy of the authority figure issuing the directive may be extremely clear.

Legitimacy of the authority figure may involve the relationship of a perpetrator to the child. It seems likely that children attribute less legitimacy to strangers than to relatives or adults occupying socially sanctioned authority roles. Based on this premise, one would predict that children would find resisting and reporting inappropriate actions of a relative much more difficult than responding to a stranger. The stranger may be seen by the child as having little legitimate authority.

Another implication of legitimacy involves the child's ability to discriminate between legitimate and illegitimate directives. What do children perceive as "wrong" in the domain of adult authority? Damon (1977) maintained that blatantly immoral directives are readily identified by children as young as age 4. Children issued an illegitimate directive are able to state that they do not have to obey. Thus, even young children know that a grown-up has the right to tell them to pick up toys, but does not have the right to tell them to steal from a store.

What, then, of sexually abusive directives and advances? Even a young child directed to perform an obviously deviant act may readily identify the directive as an illegitimate use of authority, a clear breach of an authority figure's realm. Bogat and McGrath (1993), using Damon's Authority Questions and the "What-If Situations Test," determined that young children achieved higher authority reasoning on the sexual abuse vignette than in the vignette describing a parent directing a child to clean his or her room. No correlation between authority reasoning levels for the two stories was established. This finding means that the children appeared to have higher reasoning abilities about sexual abuse than about other adult authority. However, a possible explanation for these findings has to do with the language contained in the sexual abuse story.

The sexual abuse story involves a perpetrator who states to a child, "Mark, if you pull down your pants and let me touch your private parts, I'll give you new crayons and coloring books" (Bogat & McGrath, 1993, p. 655). Following Damon's observations that even young children recognize blatant misuses of adult authority, it seems likely that many children told to "pull down your pants and let me touch your private parts" would refuse. However, such refusals, like the findings of the Bogat and McGrath study, should be considered minimally reassuring.

In reality, less overt sexual advances, such as tickling and touching "games" that are unfamiliar, confusing, or stimulating for the child, may fail to trigger even an older child's awareness of the directive's illegitimacy or the child's right to disobey the perpetrator. Bogat and McGrath (1993) suggested that the children in their study demonstrated higher authority reasoning levels on the abuse story than on the benign story because the "children seemed to understand that this was a moral situation . . . a violation of a moral code" (p. 658). An alternative explanation, however, is that many of the children automatically responded to the "red flag" of words such as *private parts* and *pulling down pants*, and thus only appeared to reason at a higher level by providing a socially conforming response without underlying rationale. The discrepancy between a child's more realistic level of authority reasoning, as demonstrated by responses to the benign vignette, and the inflated authority reasoning that may have been an artifact of the way the story was worded may explain the lack of correlation between the two measures of authority reasoning.

As children grow older and develop increased social reasoning, they construct their own rationales for obedience. The construction process includes evaluating all directives for their merit and legitimacy. Much to parents' frustration, the safety warning "Don't get in a car with a stranger" may undergo the same childhood scrutiny as the more benign directive "Don't wear the same underwear two days in a row." Children indulge their developmentally appropriate urges to evaluate, question, defy, and reject even important safety directives, simply in the service of testing out newly developed authority reasoning capabilities.

THE DEVELOPMENT OF
INTERPERSONAL UNDERSTANDING

Another area of social cognition that may offer insight into children's vulnerability to sexual abuse involves the development of interpersonal understanding. Children grow in their ability to understand themselves, others, and themselves in relationship to others. The development of reasoning about human actions and intentions occurs slowly, influenced, no doubt, by both maturational and environmental forces.

In a landmark study, Flapan (1968) designed a project to investigate children's understanding of interpersonal relationships. She interviewed children at three age levels (6, 9, and 12) after showing them film clips depicting social interactions. The subjects' spontaneous responses and answers to structured interview questions were recorded and classified as descriptive, explanatory, or interpretative. Flapan's findings suggest developmental trends in the way children recall behavior sequences. The younger subjects relied heavily on description, and were likely to recall obvious, observable features of a social interaction (i.e., "She cried"). The older age groups also used descriptive terms but were able to employ inference to report their ideas about unobservable features of the story they viewed (i.e., "She was sad"). The younger children were literal and concrete in their interpretations of events, and gave virtually no psychological explanations for events depicted. A typical 6-year-old's response was, "She cried because the squirrel was dead." An older subject was likely to include a psychological explanation such as, "She cried because she felt sad." The highest level of social cognition—inference in interpersonal relationships—was found infrequently and only among the oldest subjects (i.e., "She cried because he made her feel bad"). Flapan (1968) identified the span from age 6 to age 9 as an important "transition phase" in the development of interpersonal understanding.

The development of interpersonal understanding, from the recounting of concrete features of social interaction to the ability to detect emotional states, suggests how social cognition unfolds, with a positive correlation between social awareness and chronological age. She, like Damon, noted a transition phase, between ages 6 and 9, that involved dramatic, although uneven, acquisition of social awareness.

As social cognition develops, the child's social sphere expands and becomes more complex. New awareness of others beyond self allows the child to reflect on previously unnoticed social interactions. The Piagetian concept of children not merely gaining more knowledge, but acquiring different ways of knowing, may be a feature of social cognitive growth (Piaget, 1970).

GROWING AWARENESS OF SELF AND OTHERS

Selman (1980) identified five stages of social cognitive development that span childhood from preschool to late adolescence. Selman proposed that understanding interpersonal interactions involves social perspective taking, which begins with an awareness that self has a point of view and moves to the awareness that other also has a point of view. Social perspective taking includes the ability to infer the psychological states of others.

Stage 0

The first stage of interpersonal understanding, Stage 0, reflects "undifferentiated and egocentric perspective taking" (Selman, 1980, p. 37). The young child, between ages 3 and 6, is unable to distinguish between self and others as distinct "psychological entities" or to differentiate between acts and feelings. In relationships with others, the Stage 0 thinker believes others to feel as he or she feels, and to want what he or she wants.

Stage 1

Stage 1 reasoning introduces the concept that self and other may differ in terms of subjective state, but the ability to infer such differences is limited to only the obvious. Between ages 5 and 9, interpersonal interactions are understood in single dimensions (e.g., giving a gift always makes someone happy) or as one-way endeavors (e.g., "She likes me because she helps me").

Stage 2

Stage 2 reasoning, ages 7–12, involves a growing capacity to step outside oneself for self-reflection or to take another's perspective. Psychological inference aids interpersonal understanding, and the Stage 2 child realizes that outward appearance and inner reality may not be the same.

Stage 3

Social perspective taking at Stage 3 includes the ability to see self, other, and self–other in relation to each other. The Stage 3 reasoner, ages 10–15, realizes that relationships depend not only on the functioning of self or other, but on how the two interact.

Stage 4

Stage 4 reasoning, ages 12 through adulthood, introduces two new concepts. First, there is a realization that even self may not fully know or understand self. Selman (1980) referred to this as the "generation of a notion of the unconscious." The second concept is the individual's awareness that personality is a product of a person's traits, beliefs, values, and attitudes (Selman, 1980). The ability to envision relationships on an abstract level emerges, enabling an individual to assume the perspectives taken by society in general.

In a study including 225 subjects ranging in age from 2 to 32 years, Selman (1980) found much broader age ranges than he had proposed. Stage 0 reasoning was found in children ages 2 years 4 months through 5 years 11 months. Stage 1 reasoning was found in children from ages 4 years 6 months through 12 years 4 months. Stage 2 reasoning was found in children ages 6 years 9 months through 15 years 10 months. Stage 3 reasoning was in evidence in people ranging in age from 11 years 3 months through adulthood. Stage 4 reasoning appeared no sooner than 17 years 8 months, and continued to be in evidence through adulthood.

CHILDREN'S UNDERSTANDING OF PARENTS

Selman (1980) investigated peer interactions, childhood friendship, and the development of self-knowledge. In conjunction with Selman's work, Bruss-Saunders (1979) investigated children's interpersonal functioning with parents. Selman incorporated Bruss-Saunders' findings with his own, and her measure, The Parent–Child Interview, became part of Selman's comprehensive assessment of children's social reasoning. The combined work of Selman and Bruss-Saunders sheds light on children's social reasoning about a particular category of adult: parents.

SOCIAL REASONING ABOUT PARENTS

Bruss-Saunders (1979) conducted interviews with 118 children, ranging in age from 6 to 18 years. The interview consisted of a short story describing a common childhood dilemma: to obey or not to obey. Each child was asked a standard set of interview questions to determine the reasons underlying his or her responses. Questions were formulated to assess five major areas of parent–child relations: (a) relationship formation, or how the child defines the nature of the parent–child bond; (b) love and cooperation; (c) obedience, or why children have to obey their parents; (d) punishment, or what gives parents the right to punish their children; and (e) conflict and conflict resolution, or what causes children and parents to fight, and how they reconcile after conflict.

Selman and Bruss-Saunders found that children's understanding of the parent–child relationship becomes increasingly sophisticated with age. The beginning reasoning levels reflect the egocentric logic of the preoperational stage thinker. The advanced levels incorporate the egocentric perspective of self with an emerging awareness that others can and do have different perspectives.

STAGES OF REASONING AND
SOURCES OF VULNERABILITY

A child's understanding of others and the relationship between self and others may create an additional source of vulnerability to sexual abuse. Characteristics of normal social cognitive development include limitations in social awareness and a tendency to overapply emerging abilities. Reasoning "deficits" may render many children cognitively vulnerable to the perpetrator's sophisticated social reasoning tactics.

Stage 0 Reasoning

Stage 0 reasoning, typically found in children by age 3, reflects the young child's egocentric and pragmatic conception of the world, including the parent–child relationship (Selman, 1980; Selman, Jaquette, & Bruss-Saunders, 1979). The parent–child relationship is easily defined: Mom and Dad care for me because they are my parents. Children should obey parents because they are the parents. Good children are good because they are rewarded. Such circularity of logic defines the function of punishment: Children are punished because they are bad and children are bad because they are punished. There is no understanding of the causes of conflict, and conflict resolution is accomplished by (a) physically removing oneself from the unpleasant situation, or (b) forgetting about the conflict. The end of a fight signals the end of conflict for the Stage 0 thinker.

In terms of vulnerability to a perpetrator, the Stage 0 reasoner maintains that reward is an affirmation of goodness. Candy, special favors, praise, and affection may win a young child's compliance with abuse, not solely for the purpose of enjoying the offered item, but also because the child believes that, just as good children are rewarded, rewarded children are good. Complying with an inappropriate directive that ends with the child receiving treats may lead the child to see him- or herself as good simply because the treat was given. A lollipop or colorful sticker given to a child at the doctor's office following a painful injection is based on this commonly observed feature of early childhood: A child can endure fear, discomfort, uncertainty, or pain and then be placated with a tangible reward. The reward signals to the child, "You are good because you got something good." It is likely that some perpetrators of abuse against young children exploit the normal circular logic that characterizes this earliest stage of social reasoning.

Unquestioned obedience to authority appears to be typical at this age. Healthy, developmentally appropriate children may be quite vulnerable to obeying, without question, when told to do anything, whether good or bad, comfortable or uncomfortable. Stage 0 reasoners do not see punishment as contingent upon social behavior or intentions. A child who is punished because mother or father is in a bad mood is as equally deserving of punishment as a child who is punished for deliberate disobedience. Threats of harm, force, betrayal, abandonment, and rejection are likely to be totally believable for Stage 0 youngsters, who are incapable of assessing how punishments are related to misdeeds. A Stage 0 child threatened with "I'll tell your parents and they'll know what a bad child you were" may find that threat not only "logical," but also justifiable. The Stage 0 child may believe that he or she deserves to be punished if an adult tells the child he or she is bad.

Stage 0 reasoners do not understand conflict; they know only it is to be avoided or forgotten. Encouraging a young child to report a sexually abusive encounter appears to be in opposition to the naturally occurring tendency at this stage to resolve conflict by forgetting about it. The other method of conflict resolution—avoidance of conflict situations—may serve as at least partial protection for young children. Unlike their more socially aware elders, young children are capable of fleeing or escaping without concern for social appearance. The same "boorishness" that enables a young child to unabashedly refuse to play with a friend who broke a treasured toy allows a Stage 0 child to reject anyone associated with conflict.

Implications of Stage 0 reasoning for the reporting of perpetrators are troubling. Once the conflict situation is terminated, the conflict is over and resolved in the young child's mind. Motivation "to tell" may be minimal for a child in this stage, perhaps because he or she fears punishment and wishes to avoid getting in trouble, but also because, if the perpetrator has been successfully "avoided," the Stage 0 child may reason that the conflict is over.

Previous research conducted by Burkhardt (1986) found that 4- and 5-year-old children were more likely to physically flee from a stranger who asked them to help than 6- and 7-year-old subjects, who tended to rely on verbal avoidance tactics. However, across age groups, the majority of these young children (more than 80% of 103 subjects) did not report the encounter with the stranger to a nearby teacher, perhaps because they had managed to successfully escape the unfamiliar perpetrator.

Stage 1 Reasoning

Stage 1 reflects movement toward logic as a means of explaining interpersonal relationships. The reasoning may be of the simplest type: The parent deserves obedience, love, cooperation, and the right to punish because the parent knows best. Goodness and justice are dispensed by good and just adults. Stage 1 children display a sensitivity to the inferiority of their position: Children need and deserve punishment to be protected, taught a lesson, or "paid back" for an infraction. Punishment is to be avoided by obedience, and conflict is resolved by one party appeasing or giving in to the other. Good children owe their elders gratitude and obedience, with obedience seen as a sign of love for parents.

Developmental factors may impinge upon a Stage 1 child's ability to resist and report an adult perpetrator. A child realizes that "self" is impacted upon by social factors, such as "I am *bad* if I do not obey or help." A stranger's invitation to assist in finding a lost puppy or an incestuous father's request to help Daddy "feel better" may be seen by the child as a social opportunity to earn the status of "good child." Even if the request defies the child's own wishes, the Stage 1 reasoner is fully immersed in the subjugation of egocentric self. Conforming to the specifications of others is typical for this stage.

Obedience for its own sake, and in the service of avoidance of punishment, is characteristic of Stage 1. A child directed to comply with even an abusive request may obey simply to avoid being punished for noncompliance. Once Stage 1 children experience blame or punishment, they are likely to believe that such punishment is fully deserved because they lack the reasoning ability to disconfirm their own hypotheses. In a similar vein, the Stage 1 child is susceptible to threats of punishment or blame. A perpetrator's accusation that the child is responsible for the things that have happened may be utterly convincing to a Stage 1 reasoner.

The confusion of Stage 0 (i.e., "I do not know why this conflict happened") may be replaced with a rationale that is all too certain of the reason this conflict happened (i.e., "because of *me*"). Conflict can best be resolved by appeasement, as the Stage 1 reasoner believes that giving in is associated with being good. The composite vulnerability of a Stage 1 child includes vulnerability in several areas: adults know best, punishment is deserved, and punishment and conflict are avoided by compliance and appeasement.

Stage 2 Reasoning

Tenets of Stage 2 include children's view of parents as reliable guardians who are sensitive to the needs of children. Parents who love their children are concerned with the children's feelings as well as their physical care. Lack of parental sensitivity is believed to be a sign of lack of love for the child. For the first time, parents are not seen as all-knowing; parents are not always right. Obedience to parents serves to prevent upsetting the emotional balance of the relationship. The concept of *punishment* is questioned by the Stage 2 child. While the child believes that the parent intends punishment to be beneficial, either as a lesson or a deterrent, the child is skeptical as to whether punishment really achieves this end. Conflict is believed to stem from differences of opinion, rather than the pitting of right against wrong. Therefore, conflict can be resolved by understanding each other or using an arbitrator. There is a recognition that conflict cannot always be resolved, but that it can be ended by letting the other party win.

The perspective-taking abilities of Stage 2 open up a new world to the child—the world of "other." Throughout Stages 0 and 1, the child grew in understanding of self, labeling others' behavior as somehow related to self. Stage 2 marks the advent of the child's ability to maintain a sense of psychological self as separate and distinct from others. Parents, too, are seen as psychological beings. Relationships are believed to be mutually beneficial and should contribute to the happiness of each party. Punishment loses some of its overwhelming power as the child becomes aware that its application may alter the child's overt behavior, but is powerless to affect the inner processes such as attitudes, beliefs, and feelings.

Stage 2 reasoning may offer some resilience to children encountering a perpetrator. Adults are no longer viewed as always "knowing best," particularly if the child does not experience the adult's actions as emotionally supportive. A Stage 2 child who feels unhappy or angry may be less likely to feel responsible for, or deserving of, unpleasant feelings. In fact, the Stage 2 child may experience his or her own distress as a sign of lack of love or caring on the part of the adult. Caregivers of school-age children are, perhaps, most familiar with the typical parent–child exchange in which a 10-year-old child responds with "You don't love me" when denied a request or privilege. Selecting gifts for the Stage 2 child may be more difficult than for the younger child, as the older child feels affirmed of being loved if the gift is pleasing. In terms of vulnerability to sexual abuse, the Stage 2 child may be more judgmental regarding a perpetrator's intentions and more difficult to placate than a younger child.

At the same time, Stage 2 carries with it some potential sources of vulnerability. The child may still comply with adult directives to avoid causing conflict and upsetting the adult, using such compliance as a means to avoid conflict. Further, a Stage 2 child, while capable of soliciting arbitration to resolve a conflict, might report a perpetrator if the abusive situation is ongoing, but might fail to report an encounter that the child believes has been sufficiently resolved.

Stage 3 Reasoning

Stage 3 reasoning includes a child's belief that love between parent and children is reciprocal and psychological in nature. Children are a source of pride for parents; parents are a source of security for children. Good parents wish to foster their children's growth and independence, and are willing to tolerate their children's wishes, even if those wishes do not coincide with their own. At the same time, good children are sensitive to their parents' feelings, and have a sense of responsibility to parents that stems from respect and appreciation, rather than indebtedness. For the first time, love between parents and children is understood in psychological terms, and is associated with closeness, trust, respect, and forgiveness of each party for the other. Sensitivity to each one's needs and opinions emerges as an important feature in the parent–child relationship.

A parent's exercise of authority is seen as a function of the parent's need to feel in control or to be treated with respect, rather than as a helpful means of interacting with a child. Obedience is seen by the Stage 3 reasoner as good for young children, but not particularly relevant to the adolescent, whose primary focus is interacting with peers. Punishment is viewed as a mechanism that ineffective parents resort to when they feel out of control.

The Stage 3 child moves away from being the passive recipient of a parent's anger or lecture. The child moves toward being the owner of his or her feelings and experiences. Conflict is caused by differences in opinion, rather than disobedience. For example, a Stage 3 child may state, "You think I need to be in by midnight but I don't think so," belying a logic that maintains that curfews, like favorite pizza toppings, are selected. Stage 3 children are aware that conflict occurs even when both parties love each other; for the first time, conflict is not viewed as necessarily somebody's fault. Conflict resolution reflects this non-judgmental view because the Stage 3 reasoner conflict can only truly be resolved by compromise and acceptance of differences. Additionally, there is a realization that not all conflict can be resolved.

Stage 3 reasoning reflects major movement away from childhood dominance by adult authority. These changes may make the child less compliant with many exercises of adult authority, whether the directives are legitimate or abusive. The Stage 3 child may realize that a perpetrator holds a particular opinion, but the child would not feel compelled to comply with directives emanating from that opinion. Stage 3 children believe themselves entitled to their own opinions and free to determine their own actions. Threats of punishment or fear of creating conflict fail to trouble the Stage 3 reasoner, who has grown to accept such happenings as facts of adult life. By Stage 3, social reasoning has developed to a point at which autonomy is more valued than compliance.

A perpetrator's mere position of authority over the authority-defying Stage 3 child is not likely to be a major contributing factor to adolescent sexual abuse. However, a possible source of vulnerability may be related to Stage 3 thinking. These teens are engrossed in the age-appropriate tasks of exploring the terms of their own sexuality. At the same time, their interpersonal relationships with adults are based on the adults' tolerance of the teens' opinions, feelings, and behavior. A Stage 3 child may be led into a sexual relationship with a perpetrator who gains the child's respect by tolerating an authority-defying teen's behaviors, such as drinking, drug use, truancy, or runaway. Some circumstances of statutory rape, prostitution, and teen involvement in pornography production may be examples of adolescent vulnerability to sexual exploitation.

Although a comprehensive look at the subject of adolescent sexuality is beyond the scope of the present topic, it should be noted that much of the sexual activity associated with adolescence is neither considered abusive by society in general nor by the teens themselves. Finkelhor (1979) suggested that sexual activity between teens and significantly older persons may be perceived by children as experimentation, rather than abuse. Although concerned parents may attempt to protect teens from sexual activity with older, more experienced individuals, the reasoning of Stage 3 teens may lead them to believe that they are quite capable of making informed choices about social activities, including sex.

STAGES OF REASONING AND AGE NORMS

In fact, older children in the age range of 15–18 continue to display Stage 1 reasoning. Socioeconomic factors were suggested by Bruss-Saunders as a possible source of delayed social reasoning, although no mechanism for such a delay was described. In general, however, Selman and Bruss-Saunders found age and social reasoning to be positively correlated; that is, as chronological age increased, social reasoning ability also increased.

SOCIAL COGNITION AND
VULNERABILITY TO SEXUAL ABUSE

It seems likely that developmental, social, emotional, and cultural factors interact to create varying degrees of vulnerability to childhood sexual abuse. Chronological age may influence social norms regarding the amount of supervision given a child. Social cognitive development may affect the degree of preparedness the child possesses for recognizing and responding to various social demands, regardless of age. Biological factors, such as attractiveness and pubescence, may affect the manner in which others approach and interact with a child. Emotional features, such as depression, anxiety, feelings of rejection, low self-esteem, or thrill-seeking, may predispose some children to barter sexual contact in exchange for comfort, escape, or validation. One can imagine substantial vulnerability to sexual abuse for an attractive, pubescent adolescent with Stage 1 reasoning, whose culture affords the opportunity to spend unsupervised time with potential perpetrators. If this child manifests emotional disturbance or behavioral disorder in interpersonal functioning, an even greater degree of vulnerability may be expected.

SUMMARY

Chapter 2 discussed various factors that make children vulnerable to childhood sexual abuse, including intrapsychic, biological, social, and familial contributions. Theories pertaining to children's vulnerability have minimized developmental contributions. Limited social reasoning, which is a normal part of childhood, may put children at particular disadvantage in responding to an adult perpetrator. Damon (1977) determined that authority reasoning emerges and changes throughout childhood. Selman (1980) and Bruss-Saunders (1979) established that interpersonal understanding and reasoning about parents are characterized by increasing awareness of the relationship between self and others. A link between normal childhood social reasoning and vulnerability to sexual abuse was described.

Chapter 3

Vulnerability to Childhood Sexual Abuse as a Function of Social Reasoning

Chapters 1 and 2 defined the problem of childhood sexual abuse and possible developmental contributions to vulnerability, including the ways children think and reason about adults. Chapter 3 begins with a general discussion of research methods for studying children's social reasoning, and culminates with the details of a specific child-generated model of sexual abuse intervention. Features of childhood reasoning about adults, including perpetrators, are presented.

SOCIAL REASONING RESEARCH

Social reasoning research, much like social reasoning itself, is simultaneously simple and complex. It is simple in that it focuses on that which is ordinary: people's thoughts about themselves and others. Yet there is complexity in detecting patterns among the myriad ways in which people become interpersonally aware and active, and the ways in which awareness and activity change over time and circumstance. Social reasoning research, simple in its methods yet complex in the implications of its findings, affords the concerned adult a means to better understand a child's view of the social world.

SOCIAL REASONING METHODOLOGY

Measures of children's social reasoning about adults typically include an interview during which children are read hypothetical situations and then asked questions. For girls, the stories contain a main character who is a girl of the same age as the subjects. For boys, the main character is described as a boy of their same age. In each story, there is some type of social dilemma involving an adult and the main character. The children offer spontaneous ideas about the circumstances described in the stories and possible responses to those situations. Interview questions are designed to probe the children's reasons for their answers. Responses are scored for level of social reasoning based on criteria developed by the authors of the interviews.

THE AUTHORITY INTERVIEW

The Authority Interview, developed by Damon (1977), includes a story in which the main character faces being told to do something that he or she does not want to do such as cleaning, something morally wrong such as stealing, or something that is unfair such as staying inside because a parent is in a bad mood. The child is questioned about the rights of the authority figures and the main character in the story. A low scoring response would be: "The kid has to do what the parent says or else he won't have a parent and will die because he won't have any food or place to live." A higher level response might be: "The parent should not tell the kid to do that because it is wrong and against the law." Using criteria developed by Damon, responses to the Authority Interview are scored for a level of reasoning about adult authority.

Damon described characteristics of children's reasoning about authority at three levels (see chap. 2). The general findings of the Damon study include a positive correlation between social reasoning and chronological age. No differences in social reasoning ability between boys and girls were detected.

THE STORY OF JANE/JIMMY

The Story of Jane/Jimmy was one of several interviews developed by Bruss-Saunders (1979) to investigate children's social reasoning about parents. The interview begins with a story about a child who has to decide whether to follow a parent's instructions. For example, a child wants to buy a toy, but the parent has indicated the child should not buy the toy. The interview questions were intended to uncover the subject's understanding of parental authority, obedience, punishment, and parent–child conflict. Examples of typical interview questions are: Should Jane obey her mother? Why? Why do you think parents punish their children? A child responding to these questions with statements like "Jane should obey because her parent is the parent" and "Kids should get punished so that they don't do it" would be scored at a lower level of social reasoning than a child responding with, "Kids should obey because the parent is older and knows what to tell her so that she can learn." Using scoring criteria developed by Selman et al. (1979) and based on Bruss-Saunders' study, responses to *The Story of Jane/Jimmy* are assigned social reasoning scores.

Bruss-Saunders and Selman et al. provided detailed descriptions of the characteristics of children's reasoning about parents in 10 areas, such as parents' motives for having children, children's needs for parents, punishment, and obedience. Bruss-Saunders described "age related changes in children's ways of thinking about parental behavior and the parent–child relationship" based on "Selman's developmental stages of social perspective-taking ability" (Bruss-Saunders, 1979, p. 61). Her findings include support for a positive correlation between chronological age and stage of social reasoning about the parent–child relationship. She also outlined a comparison of her stages of reasoning about parents with Damon's levels of reasoning about authority. No differences between boys and girls in terms of the development of social reasoning about parents were reported.

THE BURKHARDT STUDY

The Burkhardt study included three measures of social reasoning. In addition to *The Story of Jane/Jimmy* (Bruss-Saunders, 1979) and the Authority Interview (Damon, 1977), a Perpetrator Interview (Burkhardt, 1991) was written specifically for this study. Modeled after the interviews generally used in social reasoning research, the Perpetrator Interview used many of the same questions used in *The Story of Jane/Jimmy* and the Authority Interview.

Incorporating the other authors' questions into the Perpetrator Interview was essential. Damon, Bruss-Saunders, and Selman developed extensive scoring criteria for estimating social reasoning. To apply their scoring criteria to the children's responses to the Perpetrator Interview, it was necessary to ask at least some of the same questions. In this way, exploration of children's social reasoning about perpetrators could be grounded in methods and findings already established as pertinent to normal childhood development.

SOCIAL REASONING AND VULNERABILITY

The Burkhardt study investigated a possible association between social reasoning and vulnerability to childhood sexual abuse. In this context, *social reasoning* was defined as the characteristics of children's thoughts about adults, including perpetrators. In the Burkhardt study, *vulnerability to childhood sexual abuse*, a broad and abstract concept, was reduced to practical and measurable terms: children's capacities to think of responses to inappropriate adult actions. A "less vulnerable" child might show that he or she recognizes the inappropriateness of an adult's actions (recognition), has good ideas about how to resist the adult (resistance), and is eager and willing to tell someone about what happened (reporting). A "more vulnerable" child might fail to recognize potentially abusive adult actions, offer little or no resistance to the adult, and keep the interaction a secret.

Children who lack the underlying logic needed to make a connection between what to do and when to do it will continue to be vulnerable to sexual abuse, despite practice, instructions, and warnings. Prevention efforts, predominantly "adult generated," are based on adult ideas of what children should do. However, telling a child how to respond to a perpetrator and then hearing the child reassuringly echo the instructor's script on cue may go far to soothe concerned parents and teachers, but do little to offer the child genuine help in an actual encounter with a perpetrator. The deterioration in prevention education noted elsewhere (Melton, 1992a; Wurtele & Miller-Perrin, 1992) may be due to the possibility that, after prevention education is completed, children revert to thinking about adults, including perpetrators, in their old, familiar, developmentally appropriate ways. Further, once caregivers are content that a child knows how to respond, they may be less protective of the child because they rely on their belief that the child knows how to take care of him- or herself.

GOALS OF A CHILD-GENERATED MODEL OF SEXUAL ABUSE INTERVENTION

A type of developmental vulnerability based on the gap between what children may know and what they understand was expected to emerge in the children's responses to the Perpetrator Interview. The purposes of exploring developmental vulnerability were: (a) to determine to what extent normal children display vulnerability to sexual abuse, (b) to tap children's reasoning capabilities about perpetrators, and (c) to accumulate child-generated strategies for recognizing, resisting, and reporting perpetrators. The goals of a child-generated model of sexual abuse intervention are as follows:

1   to acquire information about what and how children think about adults, in general, and perpetrators, in particular
2   to inventory children's own strategies for responding to perpetrators
3   to document children's underlying logic for the strategies they identify
4   to use the information provided by children to guide the selection of techniques for prevention and treatment of sexual abuse.

THE PERPETRATOR INTERVIEW

The stories written for the Perpetrator Interview involved situations with adults who made inappropriate actions toward children (Table 3.1). The Perpetrator Interview was written with three versions, each containing a different type of perpetrator: an uncle, a coach, and a stranger. Only male perpetrators were

Table 3.1   Perpetrator Interview

Stranger version

I am going to tell you a story about Tommy. He is a boy your age.

One day Tommy was outside playing. A man was walking by. The man stopped walking and started to talk to Tommy. The man told Tommy that he had lost his little puppy. The man said he was very sad and very worried about the dog. The man told Tommy that he was the kind of boy who could help him find the puppy.

The man told Tommy to look at a picture of the little lost puppy. While he showed Tommy the picture, the man knelt close to Tommy and put his hand on Tommy's bottom.

Coach version

I am going to tell you a story about Tammy. She is a girl your age.

In the summer, Tammy was on a baseball team. Her coach's name was Mr. Z. One day Mr. Z said that he needed a special helper to help him. She was very happy when Mr. Z picked her. Mr. Z told Tammy to put all the baseballs and bats in a big basket.

Tammy carried the basket to a little room near the baseball field. Mr. Z went into the room with Tammy. In the room, Mr. Z knelt down close to Tammy and put his hand on her bottom.

Uncle version

I am going to tell you a story about Tommy. He is a boy your age.

One night Tommy's uncle told him to turn off the TV and get ready for bed. His uncle came into Tommy's room to tell him goodnight. They talked about school. Tommy said he had a good day. His uncle said he had a bad day and had many things to do. He told Tommy he liked to talk to Tommy because, out of all the kids, Tommy was the best.

Tommy's uncle sat on the bed close to Tommy. As he talked, he put his hand on Tommy's bottom.

---

included, based on the findings by Finkelhor (1986) that child molesters are most frequently men.

Although the three versions of the Perpetrator Interview are fictional, they are composites of actual child–perpetrator encounters described by individuals who experienced childhood sexual abuse. Descriptions reported by Bass and Davis (1988), Finkelhor (1984), and Rush (1980) detail actual circumstances of sexual abuse, with perpetrators often befriending children to gain proximity to them, such as strangers who ask for help or family friends who want to play a new "game." Therefore, there was a deliberate effort to use realistic ways in which a child might encounter a perpetrator.

The Perpetrator Interview stories begin with a perpetrator issuing a benign or legitimate directive, such as telling the child to turn off the television (uncle), pick up sports equipment (coach), or look at a picture of a lost puppy (stranger). Each story establishes a social atmosphere by having the perpetrator engage the child in conversation. The interview story concludes with the perpetrator putting his hand on the child's "bottom."

DEFINING ABUSIVE ACTION

The action described in the Perpetrator Interview involved the perpetrator "putting his hand on the child's bottom." The selection of an inappropriate adult action for the stimulus story was made with the following considerations: (a) the need to avoid triggering automatic, socially desirable responses by the children; and (b) the desire to approximate situations associated with real perpetrator advances.

It seemed possible that children in the Burkhardt study might offer scripted responses to a perpetrator encounter if the perpetrator's abusive action was very blatant, such as telling the children to pull down their pants or saying "Let me touch your private parts." Instead, the Perpetrator Interview described an adult placing his hand on the child's "bottom," a deliberately ambiguous, but potentially inappropriate adult action. The interview was designed to first allow the children a chance to respond to this ambiguous situation. It may be important to recall that children experience uncertainty about the motives, intentions, and actions of adults in general, as described in chapter 2. Therefore, in the same vein as *The Story of Jane/Jimmy* and The Authority Interview, the Perpetrator Interview led children to make suggestions about what the main characters should do in these confusing situations, and explain the reasons for their suggestions.

As the Perpetrator Interview progressed, the children were provided with definitive information about the main character's discomfort with the perpetrator's action and desire to have the perpetrator remove his hand. Midway through the Perpetrator Interview, all children were told "Let's pretend that Tommy and his uncle do not agree about what Tommy should do. His uncle wants to touch Tommy, but Tommy wants him to stop. Can Tommy end this disagreement?" In summary, all children were given an initial opportunity to spontaneously respond to the abusive situation, then were subsequently questioned about specific features of the perpetrator story.

PREDICTIONS OF VULNERABILITY IN THE BURKHARDT STUDY

The Burkhardt study sought to demonstrate developmental vulnerability to childhood sexual abuse related to how children view adult authority, and to explore how such views may impact on children's responses to adult perpetrators. It was predicted that children's responses to the Perpetrator Interview in the Burkhardt study would reveal vulnerability associated with (a) children viewing adult perpetrators as authority figures even in the presence of abusive actions, and (b) children finding it difficult to respond to a perpetrator in a position of authority. In general, it was proposed that developmental vulnerability to childhood sexual abuse could be demonstrated in the Burkhardt study as follows:

1 Children the same age would show similar reasoning about perpetrators.

2 It would be difficult for children to think of a response to an adult perpetrator, especially one with authority.

3 Adult authority figures would be viewed by children as entitled to obedience, even when the adult perpetrated an abusive action.

In addition to children's thoughts about perpetrators, the Perpetrator Interview was designed to solicit children's ideas about ways in which a child could respond to a perpetrator. Children's ideas for responding to a hypothetical situation would be considered an estimate of the typical child's "cognitive" preparedness for combatting sexual abuse. Questions aimed at responding to a perpetrator were not found in the Damon and Bruss-Saunders interviews, and therefore were written specifically for the Perpetrator Interview.

Responding to a perpetrator was broken down into three main components: recognition, resistance, and reporting. *Recognition* was defined for the Burkhardt study as any statement that indicated that the adult in the story had behaved inappropriately toward the child. *Resistance* was defined as any behavioral or cognitive response by a child that was intended to halt the perpetrator's attempt to touch the child. *Reporting* was defined as any strategy suggested by a child for informing another person of the perpetrator's actions.

Age Predictions

It was expected that older children would be more able than younger children to respond to a perpetrator with recognition, resistance, and reporting. It was also expected that the older children would view adults as having generally less authority.

Predictions About Type of Perpetrator

Based on the premise that children are typically aware of adults as authority figures and view them as entitled to some degree of obedience, it seemed likely that the type of perpetrator (e.g., uncle, coach, stranger) would be associated with varying degrees of vulnerability.

Gender Differences

It was unknown if or how boys and girls might differ in terms of vulnerability to sexual abuse. No differences in social reasoning were detected in previous studies of social reasoning. Therefore, boys' and girls' responses to perpetrators were compared for investigatory purposes, but without a prediction of how the groups might differ.

Table 3.2   Summary of Design: The Burkhardt Study

	Perpetrator conditions			
	Stranger	Coach	Uncle	Totals
Younger (6–8 years)				
Girls	8	9	9	56
Boys	10	10	10	
Older (9–10 years 8 months)				
Girls	10	10	10	59
Boys	9	10	10	
Totals	37	39	39	115

Social Reasoning Predictions

Based on findings by Selman, Bruss-Saunders, and Damon, it was expected that the children who displayed higher levels of social reasoning, regardless of age, would be less vulnerable to perpetrators than children who displayed lower levels of social reasoning.

DESIGN OF THE BURKHARDT STUDY

The Burkhardt study applied key elements of social reasoning theory to the study of vulnerability to childhood sexual abuse. Therefore, the study was deliberately modeled after research methods used to investigate social cognition and its development in children. Each child in the Burkhardt study was administered three interviews: *The Story of Jane/Jimmy* (Bruss-Saunders, 1979), the Authority Interview (Damon, 1977), and one of the three versions (stranger, coach, or uncle) of the Perpetrator Interview.

The inclusion of the Bruss-Saunders and Damon measures made possible a comparison of children's empirically established levels of social reasoning about adult authority. The Perpetrator Interview, similar in format and questions to the other interviews, was central to evaluating children's reasoning about perpetrators. Children were individually interviewed, and their responses were transcribed, scored, and statistically analyzed.

One hundred fifteen children, ages 6–10, were recruited and grouped by age and sex, then randomly assigned to one of the three perpetrator groups. Table 3.2 summarizes the Burkhardt study's $2 \times 2 \times 3$ factorial design with *age*, *sex*, and *perpetrator condition* serving as primary independent variables.

THE CHILDREN OF THE STUDY

The children in the study were recruited from a midwestern suburban public grammar school. One hundred fifteen children were interviewed, including 56

Table 3.3 Example of a "Blind" Interview Protocol

What do you think *** will do? Why?
S/he might quit helping "P." S/he doesn't like what he's doing.
"P" touched ***'s bottom. What does *** think about that?
S/he didn't like it.
What did *** want to do when "P" touched h—?
Move away.
"P" = perpetrator; S/he = he or she; h— = him or her.

girls and 59 boys. Ninety-five percent of the children were White, and the remainder were of Middle Eastern or Hispanic descent.

Two separate age groups were recruited. The younger group consisted of 56 children, 26 girls and 30 boys, ranging in age from 6 to 8 years. The older group, 30 girls and 29 boys, ranged in age from 9 to 10 years 8 months.

Interviewing the Children

Seven female undergraduate students enrolled in a small urban college and one female graduate student served as interviewers. Administration of the three interviews took about 1 hour. *The Story of Jane/Jimmy* and the Authority Interview were alternately administered first. The Perpetrator Interview was administered last, out of concern for any negative reactions a child might have regarding the content of the Perpetrator Interview. No participants responded with distress after the Perpetrator Interview, and no interviews were discontinued due to a child's unwillingness or inability to respond to the questions. To the contrary, most of the children were highly interested, eager to answer the questions, and, at times, reluctant to end the interview session. At the conclusion of the interview session, the interviewers thanked the children for "helping us find out what children think."

Scoring the Interview Responses

After the interview phase of the project, the interviewers were trained by the researcher to serve as raters. Responses to the Perpetrator Interview were specially prepared before rating. All identifying information about the main character and perpetrator was removed, including the sex and age of the main character and the type of perpetrator (uncle, coach, stranger). Table 3.3 illustrates an excerpt of the children's responses for "blind" scoring.

The three interviews were scored independently, with raters completing the scoring of all 115 protocols for one type of interview before proceeding to the scoring of another type. This scoring procedure enabled the raters to maximize and maintain their proficiency at using each set of scoring criteria without unnecessary switching back and forth between criteria.

Analysis of Interview Data

The children's responses to the interviews were scored using both the Damon (1977) and Selman et al. (1979) criteria to assign levels or stages of social reasoning. The Damon criteria were used to evaluate the Authority Interview and the Perpetrator Interview, yielding an Authority Reasoning Level (ARL) and a Perpetrator Authority Index (PAI). The Selman et al. (1979) criteria were used to evaluate *The Story of Jane/Jimmy* and the Perpetrator Interview, yielding a Stage Score (SS) and a Perpetrator Reasoning Score (PRS). Thus, the use of empirically derived scoring criteria from previous studies of children's reasoning about parental authority made it possible to estimate the children's social reasoning abilities about perpetrator authority.

Report of Interrater Reliability

Interrater reliability is the rate of agreement between two raters' scores. It is an index of how accurately raters used the scoring criteria when scoring individual interviews. In the Burkhardt study, the rate of agreement between raters for a child's answers met or exceeded the rates reported by the original authors. Thus, it can be concluded that the raters applied the scoring criteria in a consistent manner.

CHILDREN'S REASONING ABOUT PERPETRATORS

The children's social reasoning about adults, including perpetrators, supported the prediction that children of the same age use similar levels of social reasoning about adults, including perpetrators. Social reasoning about parents and authority was found to be correlated with social reasoning about perpetrators. Older children were found to use more advanced levels of social reasoning than younger children. No difference in reasoning between boys and girls was detected.

REPLICATION OF PREVIOUS RESEARCH IN SOCIAL COGNITION

The children interviewed for the Burkhardt study in 1991 responded to the Authority Interview (Damon, 1977) and the Parent–Child Interview (Bruss-Saunders, 1979; Selman, 1980) in much the same way as children did in previous studies.

In keeping with the data analysis employed by the previous authors, the children's ages (in months) were rank ordered and paired with their respective

Table 3.4 Correlations of Social Reasoning Measures with Age in Months

	N	r	p
Comparison of age with:			
Stage Score (SS)	115	.46	<.001
Authority Reasoning Level (ARL)	115	.35	<.001

reasoning scores. Significant correlations between social reasoning levels (or stages) and chronological age were established (Table 3.4).

These findings indicate that, as children get older, the ways in which they think and reason about authority and parents change. These changes reflect increasing complexity in their reasoning about authority, with older children believing that parents do not have absolute authority over their children and that only reasonable and fair commands must be obeyed.

RESULTS OF *THE STORY OF JANE/JIMMY*

The reasoning of the children in the Burkhardt study reflected many of the same characteristics (Table 3.5) described by Bruss-Saunders (1979), with older children demonstrating more advanced levels of social reasoning about parents than younger children.

RESULTS OF THE AUTHORITY INTERVIEW

The authority reasoning of the children in the Burkhardt study reflected many of the same characteristics (Fig. 3.1) described by Damon (1977), with older children demonstrating more advanced levels of social reasoning than younger children.

COMPARISON OF *THE STORY OF JANE/JIMMY* AND THE AUTHORITY INTERVIEW

Bruss-Saunders (1979) predicted and demonstrated a positive correlation between the parent reasoning scores of her study and Damon's ARL scores. In the Burkhardt study, this correlation was replicated ($r = .55$, $p < .001$). This

Table 3.5 Stage Scores of Children in the Burkhardt Study

Stage	Frequency	%
1	90	80
2	21	20
	111	100

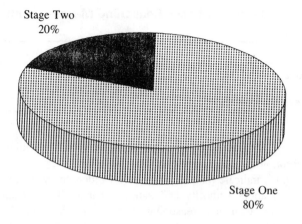

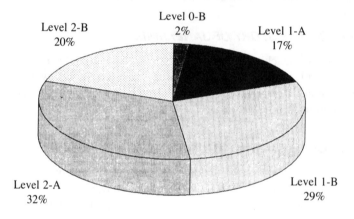

Figure 3.1   Reasoning levels of children in the Burkhardt study.

finding suggests that the stages of social reasoning about parents assessed by *The Story of Jane/Jimmy* correlate with the authority reasoning levels evaluated by the Authority Interview.

COMPARISON OF CHILDREN'S REASONING ABOUT PARENTS AND PERPETRATORS

The children's responses to the Perpetrator Interview were scored using the Damon (1977) criteria, yielding a PAI score. The Selman et al. (1979) criteria were also used to assign a PRS. Figure 3.2 details the incidence of social reasoning levels for the Perpetrator Interview using these two scoring criteria.

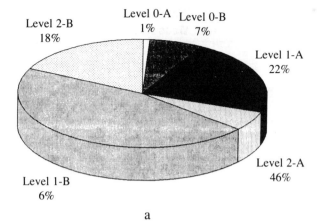

a

b

Figure 3.2 Social reasoning about perpetrators. Perpetrator Authority Index; Perpetrator Reasoning Score. Scores derived by use of the (a) Damon and (b) Selman criteria on responses to the Perpetrator Interview.

The Burkhardt study predicted a positive correlation between the way children reason about nonabusive adult authority figures and the way they reason about perpetrators. Indeed, *The Story of Jane/Jimmy* scores were positively correlated with the Perpetrator Interview scores ($r = .37$, $p < .001$; Table 3.6). The children's ARL scores were found to be positively correlated with their PAI ($r = .47$, $p < .001$).

These results indicate that the children in the Burkhardt study employed consistent reasoning in responding to both abusive and nonabusive adult authority figures.

Table 3.6   Spearman Rank-Difference Correlations: Comparisons of Nonabusive and Perpetrator Measures

	N	r	p
Comparison of:			
Stage Score (SS) with Perpetrator Reasoning Score (PRS)	111	.37	<.001
Authority Reasoning Level (ARL) with Perpetrator Authority Index (PAI)	115	.47	<.001

CONCLUSIONS

The findings regarding children's social reasoning support the conclusion that children demonstrate consistent levels of social reasoning, with the levels changing over time. The findings also support the notion that children rely on an underlying logic to understand adult authority, regardless of whether the adult is a parent or a perpetrator. This is not to say that children respond to all adult authority in the same way, but that they may reason about adult authority in a fixed way associated with the normal development of social cognition.

No significant pattern of differences between the ARL and PAI of the children was detected ($z = .4682$, $p < .64$). Forty-two children, or 37%, had identical ARLs and PAIs; for 30% of the children, their PAI was a half-stage greater than their ARL; for 33% of the children, their ARL was a half-stage greater than their PAI. No scores differed by more than one-half of a stage.

No pattern of differences between SS and PRS was detected ($z = .00$, $p < .99$). Forty-six, or 41%, of the children, received identical SS and PRS ratings. For 30%, or 33, the SS was a half-stage less than the PRS. For 32 children, or 29%, the PRS was a half-stage less than the SS. No difference greater than one-half of a stage was detected. These findings lend additional support to the proposition that children have stable and consistent reasoning about adult authority across social situations.

IMPLICATIONS OF CHILDREN'S REASONING ABOUT ADULTS

Children's capabilities of understanding adult authority may unfold along their own time line. As features of normal development, these developing capacities may be resistant to being rushed along by educational demands for advanced knowledge. The need for children to know and understand the danger of perpetrators may be more urgent than for any previous generation, but the actual pace and competence with which children acquire knowledge about people and develop social reasoning abilities about themselves and others cannot, and perhaps should not, be hurried. Adult expectations of precocious childhood wisdom, although understandable in the face of a known social threat such as childhood sexual abuse, may need to be tempered with the reality that children's development can be influenced, but not commandeered.

DIMENSIONS OF PERPETRATOR AUTHORITY

The three versions of the Perpetrator Interview (stranger, coach, and uncle) permitted comparison of children's statements about these types of perpetrators. These perpetrators were chosen, in part, because they hold differing levels of socially sanctioned authority over children. In general, a hierarchy of authority was predicted such that the children would believe that an uncle held the most authority, a coach held less authority than an uncle, and a stranger had the least authority.

Many children view adults as having some degree of authority over them. This normal childhood phenomenon was considered a possible source of vulnerability to sexual abuse. Thus, the Perpetrator Interview included questions designed to directly assess children's beliefs about authority and different categories of adult perpetrators.

The Perpetrator Interview included questions specifically included to evaluate the following dimensions of perpetrator authority:

1   Acknowledged Authority, or the children's acknowledgment that a stranger, a coach, or an uncle has authority,
2   Amount of Authority, or how much authority an adult was believed to be entitled to,
3   Disobedience Option, or the children's belief in the right to disobey an adult under certain circumstances,
4   Legitimacy Perception, or the children's distinction between abusive and nonabusive directives, and
5   Keeping the Secret, or the children's agreement with keeping an abusive action secret if told to do so by an adult.

Acknowledged Authority

Acknowledged authority was measured in terms of the number of children who acknowledged the perpetrator's right to tell a child what to do. The question used to prompt the children was: Does this adult have a right to tell a child what to do? Most of the children in the Uncle and Coach groups acknowledged the authority of those adults. Sadly, nearly one-fourth, or 24%, of the children in the Stranger group also indicated their belief that a total stranger has the right to tell a child what to do. A summary of these findings appears in Figure 3.3.

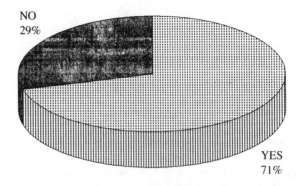

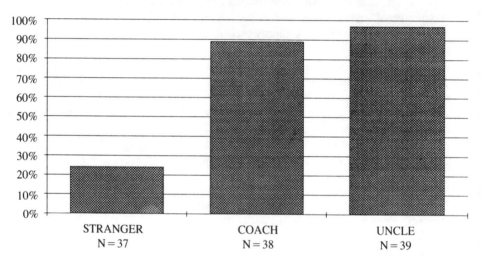

Figure 3.3   Acknowledged authority. Q: Does this adult (the perpetrator) have the right to tell a child what to do?

Amount of Authority

Amount of authority was measured by the raters, who read transcripts of the children's responses with all variable information removed, including the type of perpetrator. The raters assigned a score of 1 (*none*) to 4 (*much*) to estimate the overall amount of authority each child's responses seemed to attribute to the perpetrator. The findings regarding amount of perpetrator authority indicate that, as predicted, older children attributed less authority (mean = 2.28, *SD* = 1.03) to adults than younger children (mean = 2.73, *SD* = 1.23; Table 3.7). Additionally, the blind ratings of the children's responses reflected a hierarchy of perpetrator authority, such that an uncle (mean = 3.4) had a greater amount of

Table 3.7   Amount of Authority

Group Means and Standard Deviations for Amount of Authority Scores			
	Mean	SD	N
Stranger group	1.51	.9	37
Coach group	2.58	.89	38
Uncle group	3.39	.79	39
Younger group	2.73	1.23	56
Older group	2.28	1.03	59
Girls	2.38	1.15	55
Boys	2.62	1.15	58
Age by perpetrator			
Younger			
Stranger	1.61	1.04	18
Coach	2.79	.98	19
Uncle	3.74	.56	19
Older			
Stranger	1.42	.77	19
Coach	2.37	.76	19
Uncle	3.05	.85	19

Analysis of Variance of Amount of Authority by Age, Gender, and Type of Perpetrator		
	F	p
Main effects	25.96	.001
Age	7.22	.008
Perpetrator	46.87	.001
Sex	11.70	.20
Two-way interactions	1.08	.38
Age x Perpetrator	.95	.39
Age x Sex	2.21	.14
Perpetrator x Sex	.72	.5
Three-way interactions	.06	.94

authority than a coach [mean $= 2.6$; $t(73) = 4.23$] and a coach had a greater amount of authority than a stranger [mean $= 1.5$; $t(73) = 5.15$; $p < .001$].

Consistent with the developmental trend noted by Damon (1977) regarding children's understanding of authority, these findings indicate that older children attribute less authority to adult perpetrators than younger children.

The children of the study demonstrated an ability to distinguish among various categories of adults in terms of the amount of authority these adults were believed to have over children. This finding is important because it supports the claim that children have social reasoning capacities that underlie their interactions with adults, including perpetrators. No difference between the boys (mean =

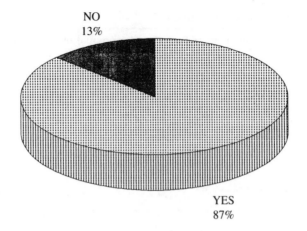

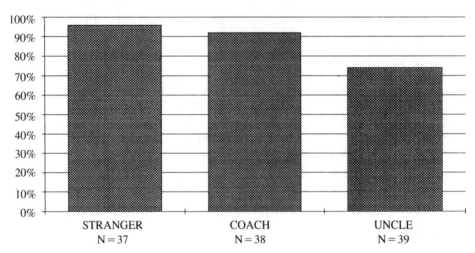

Figure 3.4   Disobedience option. Q: Does this child have a right to disobey an adult?

2.62) and girls (mean = 2.38) in the study was detected regarding the amount of authority attributed to the perpetrator in the story.

Disobedience Option

Perpetrator authority was also assessed by determining if children considered a disobedience option by agreeing that a child has a right to disobey in certain circumstances. Children were posed this question: Does a child have a right to disobey this adult? (see Fig. 3.4). Children were less likely to endorse disobeying an uncle than a stranger or a coach. No significant difference between a stranger and a coach was detected.

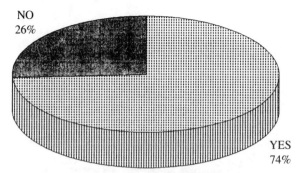

NO
26%

YES
74%

Figure 3.5 Legitimacy perception. Q: Is there a difference between the adult touching the child's bottom and the adult telling the child to do (legitimate command)?

As a point of interest, a majority of the children, or 87%, endorsed a child's right to disobey an adult. The prevalence of children's perceived right to disobey lends support to the theory that children may construct rationales about adult authority that influence their responses to adults. The formal incorporation of rationales for disobedience into prevention programs may provide a promising opportunity for using child-generated strategies for resistance.

Legitimacy Perception

The Perpetrator Interview sought to determine children's capabilities of legitimacy perception, or the ability to distinguish between legitimate and illegitimate uses of adult authority. The children were posed this question: Is there a difference between the man touching the child's bottom and the man telling the child to . . . ? (see Fig. 3.5).

Children faced with an uncle's actions were less likely to distinguish abusive from nonabusive actions than children faced with other perpetrators. Sixteen children said there was no difference between an uncle touching a child's bottom and an uncle telling a child to turn off the TV. These findings highlight the difficulties children may encounter when facing a related perpetrator.

Keeping the Secret

A final dimension of perpetrator authority had to do with the children's beliefs about keeping the secret. The question used to assess this dimension was: Pretend this man told the child *not* to tell anyone that he touched his (or her) bottom. Should the child keep that secret? Results appear in Figure 3.6.

Children told by an uncle to keep the touching a secret were four to five times more likely to agree to keep that secret (41%) than children told to keep a secret by a coach (8%) or a stranger (11%). Few children agreed to keep the coach's or stranger's actions a secret, and there was no significant difference

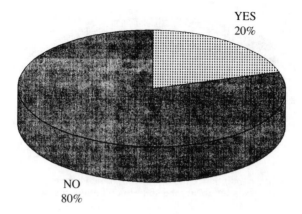

Figure 3.6   Keeping the secret. Q: Pretend the adult told the child *not* to tell anyone that he touched his (or her) bottom. Should the child keep the secret?

between these two groups. These findings have implications regarding the difficulties children experience when confronted with an offending relative.

SUMMARY

The Burkhardt study, an investigation of children's social reasoning about perpetrators, was founded in research conducted by Damon (1977), Selman (1980), and Bruss-Saunders (1979) regarding children's understanding of parents and authority. Research methods and data analysis employed by these authors served as a means to empirically link the normal development of social reasoning to children's reasoning about perpetrators of sexual abuse.

In a replication of the general findings of those earlier projects, the children of the Burkhardt study demonstrated similar characteristics of social reasoning about adults. These findings support the contention that the development of social reasoning, social perspective taking, and understanding authority occurs as a function of both maturation and social experience. Today's children continue to demonstrate the same reasoning characteristics as children 15 years ago. Nevertheless, there may be limits to how much this developmental process can be accelerated, regardless of the urgency of the need.

The children of the Burkhardt study demonstrated that they could distinguish and understand the concept of *adult authority*. They viewed the different categories of perpetrators—stranger, coach, and uncle—as possessing varying amounts of authority over children. The children also displayed the ability to distinguish between legitimate and illegitimate uses of authority, and the belief in a child's right to disobey. The demonstration of reasoning capabilities provides hope that prevention efforts, based on developmentally appropriate ways in which children think about adults, may have a good chance of arming children with useful knowledge for responding to a perpetrator.

Chapter 4

How Children Respond
to Perpetrators

Most children are told what to do if approached by a perpetrator. "Don't talk to strangers" and "Tell me if anybody tries to touch you" are common parental instructions. For certain, children are warned of many situations and expected to respond to danger by heeding those warnings. Yet teaching something does not guarantee the learning of it. "How could you do that? You *know* better!" is a refrain that probably echoed off cave walls in some equivalent version millenniums ago; it is heard in homes and schools today.

Children learn, but they do not learn all that their elders tell them. Children do not always demonstrate full understanding of what they have learned. The difference between what children have been told and what they actually know remains a constant source of frustration, worry, amazement, and amusement to adults who care for and about children.

A Biblical reference attributed to Paul in a message to the Corinthians provides one of the earliest recorded observations of the qualitative differences between the reasoning of children and adults: "When I was a child, I spoke like a child, I thought like a child, I reasoned like a child; when I became a man, I gave up childish ways" (1 Cor. 13:11).

What are the ways of a child? What does it really mean when adults expect a child "to *know* better"? The phrase implies the following: I (the adult) have already taught you (the child) about this situation. Therefore, I assume that you have learned from my teaching effort. I expect you to realize when that knowledge should be employed. I expect you to apply it whenever needed. Further, I want you to perform behaviors that logically flow from what I have taught you.

These expectations of knowledge constitute tall orders for developing minds. In chapter 3, vulnerability to childhood sexual abuse was reported in terms of children's reasoning about adult authority. In chapter 4, vulnerability is reported in terms of children's responses to perpetrators. Therefore, in addition to discovering how children think about perpetrators, the Burkhardt study sought to determine how children respond when faced with a complex social dilemma— an adult acting in an inappropriate manner. The children's responses to the Perpetrator Interview were used to assess how children react to an uncle, a coach, or a stranger who touches the former in a questionable manner.

The success of prevention education is contingent on establishing a good fit between what is being taught and the reasoning capabilities of a child at a particular age and stage of development. The Burkhardt study attempted to establish a baseline measure of children's abilities to respond to perpetrators.

DIFFERENT TYPES OF PERPETRATORS

It was a basic premise of the Burkhardt study that vulnerability to sexual abuse could be assessed by showing the children's varying responses to different types of perpetrators. Thus, the children were randomly assigned to one of three groups, with each being administered a single version of the Perpetrator Interview (uncle, coach, stranger). Three kinds of responses were evaluated: recognizing, resisting, and reporting an abusive adult action.

RECOGNITION OF PERPETRATORS

Recognition is an essential ingredient for minimizing vulnerability to sexual abuse. If a child is unable to recognize a perpetrator, the warning alarm that signals danger and triggers a protective response will not sound. Yet children face a difficult social reasoning task in recognizing inappropriate adult action because they are accustomed to doing what adults say, even when they do not understand why. In particular, the commands of adult authority figures may go virtually unscrutinized by a child who does not question an adult's right to obedience. The Perpetrator Interview provided children with an opportunity to demonstrate that they recognized inappropriate adult action.

Two types of recognition were considered: immediate recognition and prompted recognition. A child demonstrated immediate recognition of a perpetrator if, in response to the first three questions in the Perpetrator Interview, he or she indicated that the adult who put his hand on the child's bottom had acted inappropriately. Prompted recognition was scored for all children who ultimately, in any statement throughout the interview, indicated an awareness that the perpetrator was acting inappropriately.

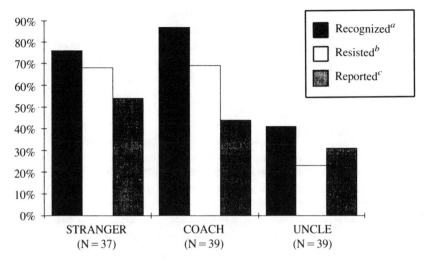

Figure 4.1 Children's immediate responses to perpetrators. *Recognized*: % of children who immediately recognized that it was inappropriate for the adult to touch a child's bottom; *Resisted*: % of children who immediately suggested resistance strategies after hearing the perpetrator story; *Reported*: % of children who immediately suggested reporting after hearing the perpetrator story.

[a]Stranger = Coach > Uncle; $p < .05$.
[b]Stranger = Coach > Uncle; $p < .05$.
[c]Stranger = Coach = Uncle; ns.

IMMEDIATE RECOGNITION

Children's immediate recognition of a perpetrator was strongly associated with the type of perpetrator (mean = 20.58; $df = 2$; $p = .00003$). The recognition rates of the children appear in Figure 4.1.

Most children interpreted the perpetrator's action, that of putting a hand on a child's bottom, as potentially abusive. Even in the Uncle group, 41% of the children thought the action was inappropriate. Therefore, it seems likely that at least some of the children who did not immediately recognize the perpetrator's action were unaware of how to respond to the situation, rather than misinterpreting the abusive action.

The children in the Uncle group were significantly less likely to recognize an uncle as a perpetrator in comparison with the children in the Stranger or Coach groups. These findings suggest that children have particular difficulty interpreting an inappropriate action by a relative in comparison with an unrelated perpetrator. One in four (25%) of the children in the Stranger group did not immediately recognize that a stranger putting his hand on a child's bottom was inappropriate.

IMMEDIATE RESISTANCE

The children's immediate resistance rates appear in Figure 4.1. Offering strategies for resisting a perpetrator was found to be associated with the type of perpetrator (mean $= 21.297$; $df = 2$; $p < .00002$). Only one in five children in the Uncle group was able to offer a resistance strategy.

These group comparisons suggest that children are less likely to offer resistance to a related perpetrator in comparison with an unrelated one. Also, 30% of the children who were told of a coach or a stranger perpetrator did not suggest immediate resistance.

IMMEDIATE REPORTING

The group differences in reporting rates were not large enough to make a conclusion regarding children's immediate reporting. In fact, many of the children from all three groups did not immediately suggest reporting (Fig. 4.1). Only about half of the children who were told of a complete stranger touching a child's bottom immediately suggested that a report should be made. Less than a third of the children in the Uncle group immediately suggested reporting an uncle.

AGE DIFFERENCES IN IMMEDIATE RESPONSE

The older children were more likely than the younger ones to recognize a perpetrator and suggest reporting him. Because chronological age is positively correlated with the development of social reasoning, it was expected that the older children (9–10 years) would demonstrate higher response rates than the younger children (6–8 years). Figure 4.2 presents the age group results for immediate responses to a perpetrator.

In terms of knowing how to immediately resist a perpetrator, the older and younger children demonstrated equivalent response rates (Fig. 4.2), with about half of the children in each group failing to offer even one resistance strategy. Thus, even when children recognize a perpetrator and may be willing to report him, they may not know how to resist him.

AGE AND TYPE OF PERPETRATOR

The type of perpetrator had a marked influence upon response rates within the two age groups (Fig. 4.3). As expected, the Uncle group had generally low recognition, resistance, and reporting rates for both age groups. However, recognition and reporting presented baffling pictures that varied within age groups.

Older Children's Responses to Perpetrators

The findings for the older age group parallel the general findings: Immediate recognition and immediate resistance of an uncle were less likely than responding to a stranger or a coach. Immediate reporting was no more predictable than the flip of a coin, even among the older children, who, one might suppose, should "know better."

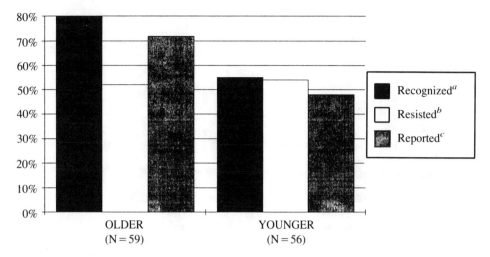

Figure 4.2 Children's immediate responses to perpetrators: older and younger groups. *Recognized*: % of children who immediately recognized that it was inappropriate for the adult to touch a child's bottom; *Resisted*: % of children who immediately suggested resistance strategies after hearing the perpetrator story; *Reported*: % of children who immediately suggested reporting after hearing the perpetrator story; *Older*: 9–10 years of age; *Younger*: 6–8 years of age.

[a]Older > Younger; $p < .05$.
[b]Older = Younger; ns.
[c]Older > Younger; $p < .05$.

Younger Children's Responses to Perpetrators

The younger children had relatively low response rates for recognizing, resisting, and reporting perpetrators. Only one in five of the younger children (21%) in the Uncle group showed recognition of an uncle's actions as inappropriate. Unexpectedly, the younger children were more likely to recognize a coach as a perpetrator than a stranger. Seven of the 18 younger children in the Stranger group (39%) did not immediately recognize that a stranger touching a child's bottom was inappropriate.

Immediate resistance by the younger children was unlikely in the Uncle group. Only one in five younger children (21%) immediately suggested even a single strategy for rebuffing an uncle. Immediate reporting, the most infrequent response to a perpetrator for both age groups, was particularly abysmal for the younger children. Only 1 of the 19 younger children (5%) in the Uncle group immediately suggested reporting the uncle's action. Although the younger children were more likely to report a coach or a stranger than an uncle, the reporting rates were still quite low. Only one in three children (33%) suggested reporting a coach, and less than half immediately said that a child should report a stranger who touches a child.

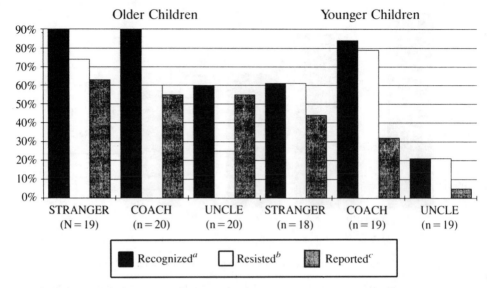

Figure 4.3 Children's immediate responses to perpetrators: age and type of perpetrator. *Recognized*: % of children who immediately recognized that it was inappropriate for the adult to touch a child's bottom; *Resisted*: % of children who immediately suggested resistance strategies after hearing the perpetrator story; *Reported*: % of children who immediately suggested reporting after hearing the perpetrator story; *Older*: 9–10 years of age; *Younger*: 6–8 years of age.

[a]Older: Stranger = Coach > Uncle, $p < .05$; Younger: Stranger < Coach > Uncle, $p < .05$.
[b]Older: Stranger = Coach > Uncle, $p < .05$; Younger: Stranger = Coach > Uncle, $p < .05$.
[c]Older: Stranger = Coach = Uncle, ns; Younger: Stranger = Coach > Uncle, $p < .05$.

The younger children could not be counted on to know how to respond to a perpetrator. As expected, the greatest difficulty was associated with the Uncle group. However, it was sobering to demonstrate that a large number of younger children did not immediately respond to what might seem, to an adult, an obviously dangerous situation—a strange man touching a child.

Review of the children's individual interviews revealed that the younger children were so focused on the problem of the lost puppy that they did not attend to what the perpetrator was doing. The demonstration of this phenomenon in a mere interview is a frightening, but realistic, portrayal of how children's social reasoning abilities are a poor match for a crafty perpetrator.

PROMPTED RESPONSES

Midpoint through the interview, all the children were told by the interviewer that the main character did not like what the perpetrator was doing, and they were then directed to provide suggestions for how the main character should respond. In other words, by the end of the interview, all children were *prompted* to: recognize that the adult's actions were wrong, suggest resistance strategies, and

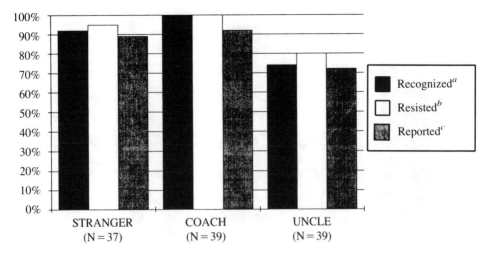

Figure 4.4 Children's prompted responses to perpetrators. *Recognized*: % of children who ultimately recognized that it was inappropriate for the adult to touch a child's bottom; *Resisted*: % of children who ultimately suggested resistance strategies after hearing the perpetrator story; *Reported*: % of children who ultimately suggested reporting after hearing the perpetrator story.

[a]Stranger < Coach > Uncle; $p < .05$.
[b]Stranger = Coach > Uncle; $p < .05$.
[c]Stranger = Coach > Uncle; $p < .05$.

agree that a report should be made. Figure 4.4 summarizes the children's rates of prompted recognition, prompted resistance, and prompted reporting.

PROMPTED RECOGNITION

Prompted recognition was scored for all children who indicated, by the end of the interview, that they knew the adult was acting inappropriately. Even after being told that the main character did not like the uncle's actions and wanted him to stop touching, 10 of the children in the Uncle group (26%) maintained that the uncle had a right to touch a child if he wanted. Of similar concern, three of the children in the Stranger group (8%), even after being prompted to recognize the abusive nature of the situation, denied there was something wrong with a stranger touching a child's bottom. (As mentioned earlier, a review of the individual interviews revealed that these children were totally focused on the problem of the lost puppy.) All of the 39 children who heard about a coach's actions recognized abuse by the end of the Coach version.

PROMPTED RESISTANCE

Prompted resistance was scored for children who, at some point in the interview, offered at least one resistance strategy. Even when directly asked for suggestions,

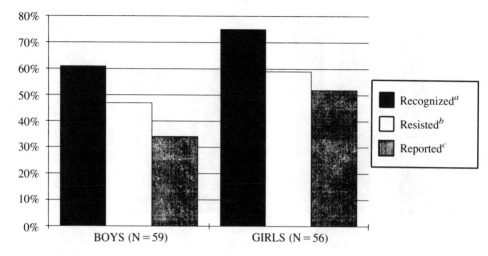

Figure 4.5 Immediate responses to perpetrators for boys and girls. *Recognized*: % of boys and girls who immediately recognized that it was inappropriate for the adult to touch a child's bottom; *Resisted*: % of boys and girls who immediately suggested resistance strategies after hearing the perpetrator story; *Reported*: % of boys and girls who immediately suggested reporting after hearing the perpetrator story.

[a]Boys = Girls; ns.
[b]Boys = Girls; ns.
[c]Boys = Girls; ns.

seven of the children in the Uncle group (20%) could not suggest a single strategy for resisting an uncle. The children were more likely to provide strategies for combatting a stranger or a coach than a related perpetrator.

PROMPTED REPORTING

Prompted reporting was accomplished by directly asking the children if the main character should tell anyone about the perpetrator. By the end of the interview, 11 of the children in the Uncle group (28%) stated "No, no one should be told about what the uncle did." As a point of information, most of these children provided rationales for their position on reporting, including fear of reprisals from parents if children told on an uncle.

Overall, reporting was less frequent than was expected or desired. About 1 in 10 children (11%) indicated that no one should be told about a stranger's actions, and 8% said no one should be told about an abusive coach.

BOYS' AND GIRLS' RESPONSES TO PERPETRATORS

No association between sex and responding to a perpetrator was discovered. Boys' and girls' rates of responding to a perpetrator appear in Figure 4.5.

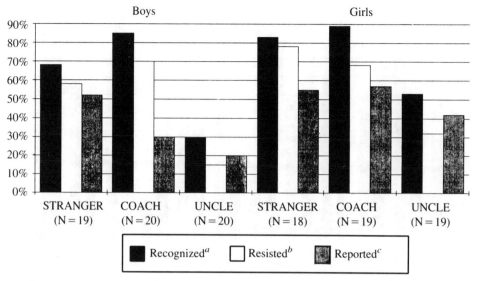

Figure 4.6 Boys' and girls' responses to perpetrators. *Recognized*: % of boys and girls who immediately recognized that it was inappropriate for the adult to touch a child's bottom; *Resisted*: % of boys and girls who immediately suggested resistance strategies after hearing the perpetrator story; *Reported*: % of boys and girls who immediately suggested reporting after hearing the perpetrator story.

[a]Boys: Stranger = Coach > Uncle, $p < .05$; Girls: Stranger < Coach > Uncle, $p < .05$.
[b]Boys: Stranger = Coach > Uncle, $p < .05$; Girls: Stranger = Coach > Uncle, $p < .05$.
[c]Boys: Stranger = Coach = Uncle, ns; Girls: Stranger = Coach = Uncle, ns.

BOYS AND GIRLS VERSUS DIFFERENT TYPES OF PERPETRATORS

For both boys and girls, the *type* of perpetrator had a marked influence on recognition and resistance rates (Fig. 4.6). Consistent with the general findings of the study, both boys and girls experienced difficulty responding to an uncle as a perpetrator. Only a third of the boys and half of the girls showed immediate recognition of an uncle's actions. In terms of immediate resistance, only 15% of the boys and 32% of the girls in the Uncle group gave an immediate suggestion for resisting. No differences in immediate reporting were detected. Both boys and girls were unlikely to recognize and resist an uncle compared with a coach or a stranger. There was no evidence of either boys or girls being more vulnerable.

SUBGROUP RESPONSES TO PERPETRATORS

For purposes of description, the response rates for older and younger boys and girls appear in Figure 4.7. Because there was a limited number of children in

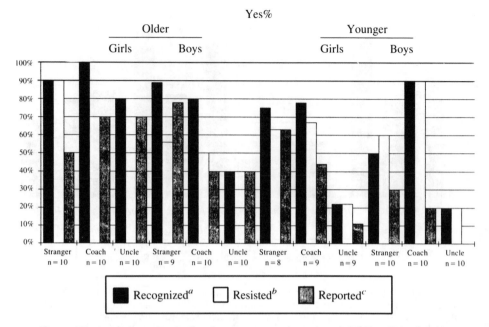

Figure 4.7 Immediate responding by age, sex, and perpetrator. [a]Older Girls: Stranger = Coach = Uncle, ns; Older Boys: Stranger = Coach < Uncle; Younger Girls: Stranger = Coach < Uncle; Younger Boys: Stranger = Coach < Uncle. [b]Older Girls: Stranger = Coach = Uncle, ns; Older Boys: Stranger = Coach = Uncle; Younger Girls: Stranger = Coach = Uncle; Younger Boys: Stranger = Coach < Uncle. [c]Older Girls: Stranger = Coach = Uncle, ns; Older Boys: Stranger = Coach = Uncle, ns; Younger Girls: Stranger = Coach = Uncle, ns; Younger Boys: Stranger = Coach = Uncle, ns.

each subgroup, inferences about the group differences are tentative. The following sections describe response findings for the four subgroups.

Older Boys

Older boys were more vulnerable to an uncle than a coach or a stranger in terms of immediate recognition. No difference in resistance and reporting was detected across the three types of perpetrators for older boys.

Older Girls

The older girls showed uniformly high (90%–100%) rates of recognition for all versions of the Perpetrator Interview. No differences in resistance or reporting rates were observed.

Younger Boys

The type of perpetrator significantly affected the younger boys' recognition abilities. Only 2 of the 10 younger boys (20%) were able to immediately recognize an uncle as a perpetrator, whereas half in the Stranger group and 90% in the Coach group immediately recognized the perpetrator's actions as inappropriate.

Younger boys in the Uncle group were also less likely to resist an uncle in comparison with a coach or a stranger. Not a single younger boy suggested reporting an abusive uncle. These findings suggest considerable vulnerability for younger boys confronted with an abusive relative.

Younger Girls

The younger girls were less likely to recognize an uncle in comparison with a stranger or a coach. One in four younger girls was unable to immediately spot a stranger or a coach as a perpetrator. No significant differences in resistance and reporting were detected for younger girls.

Considered together, these findings suggest that vulnerability to childhood sexual abuse may vary with age and sex, especially in the case of a related male perpetrator. The older boys, younger boys, and younger girls in the Uncle group had low recognition rates, much lower than the rates for the Coach and Stranger groups. Only older girls demonstrated a high recognition rate for an uncle as well as for a stranger or a coach. In general, no conclusions can be made about the children's abilities to reliably respond to a perpetrator by resisting or reporting him.

SUMMARY OF GROUP FINDINGS

The general findings of the Burkhardt study describe varying, yet real degrees of vulnerability to childhood sexual abuse as a function of the children's responses to perpetrators. The group comparisons generally support the prediction that vulnerability to sexual abuse would be greatest in an encounter with a relative. Recognizing, resisting, and reporting an uncle proved difficult for many of the children.

No statistical support was found for children responding differently to a coach or a stranger as a perpetrator. Older children, as expected, were shown to be less vulnerable to perpetrators than younger children. Boys and girls did not generally differ in their overall rates of responses to perpetrators, although uncles as perpetrators proved difficult across age and sex groups.

THE QUALITY OF CHILDREN'S RESPONSES TO PERPETRATORS

Although group comparisons provide one means to evaluate children's responses to perpetrators, numbers do not tell the entire story of children's vulnerability to sexual abuse. Children gave ''right'' answers for the wrong reasons and ''wrong'' answers for the right reasons. Some children who stated that no one should be told about an offending coach provided "reasons" for their answers. Similarly, young boys who strongly endorsed resisting often suggested "karate chopping the guy" as their defense. One little girl's resistance strategy was asking the coach "real, real nice, 'Please take your hand off my bottom.'" Thus, discussion now appropriately turns to qualitative differences in the children's responses to perpetrators.

An optimist might cite the rates of recognition, resistance, and reporting of some groups as evidence that not all children are as vulnerable as feared. Review of the actual responses to the Perpetrator Interview reveals vulnerability that statistical findings do not document. Response rates do not reflect the bravery of those children who endorsed reporting, even though they knew that punishment, reprisals, embarrassment, and disruption would be the consequences of their efforts to do the right thing. No quantitative measures belied the hopefulness of children searching for a response that might actually work, or the certainty with which many youngsters offered serious, articulate, woefully "wrong" reasons for why a child should cooperate with a perpetrator.

A child-generated model for understanding sexual abuse needs to apply children's own words as the source of the researcher's questions and answers, which are a reflection of what children really know. The children's own words allow the reader to experience the nonspecific and, perhaps, "nonquantifiable" features of their reasoning about perpetrators. Their responses to the Perpetrator Interview of the Burkhardt study are filled with many qualities: confidence, bravado, fear, uncertainty, naivete, the desire to please, and the hope of protection. In some cases, the children's words seem sorry shields pitted against the ploys of a savvy adult perpetrator. In other cases, their quick and confident statements inspire a hopefulness that prevention of sexual abuse can be accomplished.

The reader deserves a balanced view of the children's responses to social encounters involving a stranger, a coach, or an uncle touching a child in an inappropriate way. Thus, interviews that demonstrated both high and low vulnerability are included. The excerpts serve to inform the reader of the existence of, and limitations to, childhood reasoning about perpetrators.

"INVULNERABLE" CHILDREN

Adam, Older Boy, Age 9 Years 11 Months, Stranger Version

> **Interviewer:** *Tell me what you think the problem is in this story.*
> **Adam:** *That when the guy told Tommy to look for it (the dog) he should go tell his parents that he was trying to get a kid lost from his parents.*
> **I:** *What should Tommy do? Why?*

A: *Tell his parents that a stranger was telling him a story. It might not have been true and he could have gotten in trouble for taking someone's dog.*

I: *What do you think Tommy will do? Why?*

A: *He would tell his mom because he didn't think it was true about the puppy.*

I: *The man told Tommy to look at the picture of the puppy. Should Tommy do what the man said? Why or why not?*

A: *No. Cause he could have just grabbed him.*

I: *Was it OK for the man to tell Tommy to look at the picture of the dog?*

A: *No. He really shouldn't be doing nasty things.*

I: *Does a man walking down the street have the right to tell kids what to do? Why or why not?*

A: *No. Cause he's not the parents and he don't know them.*

I: *The man touched Tommy's bottom. What does Tommy think about that?*

A: *He didn't feel right about it.*

I: *What did Tommy want to do when the man touched him?*

A: *Punch him probably.*

I: *You said that Tommy should not listen to the man. Does he have a right to disobey the man?*

A: *Yes.*

I: *Do kids have the right to disobey sometimes? Like when?*

A: *The people that aren't his parents, yes, but the people that are his parents or relatives, no.*

I: *You said it was OK for Tommy to listen when the man told him to look at the picture of the puppy. You said it was not OK for the man to touch Tommy. What is the difference between those two things?*

A: *He didn't have the right for him to touch Tommy.*

I: *Is it ever OK for a kid to do what a man on the street tells him to do?*

A: *No. Sometimes, like if a policeman goes and tells them how to act if there was a fire.*

I: *What is it about a grown-up like the man on the street that would give him the right to tell a boy what to do?*

A: *The kid shouldn't listen to him.*

I: *Is it OK for a kid to obey any grown-up when the grown-up tells the kid to do something wrong? Why or why not?*

A: *No, cause he might tell him to do something nasty.*

I: *In this story let's pretend that the man and Tommy do not agree about what Tommy should do. The man wants to touch Tommy but Tommy wants the man to stop. Can Tommy end this disagreement?*

A: *Yeah. By running or by fooling him by saying "There's someone behind you" and runs into his house and tells his mom and dad.*

I: *Why wouldn't Tommy want the man to touch him?*

A: *He don't got the right to touch him.*

I: *Let's say Tommy wants to make the man stop touching him. How could he make the man stop?*

A: *By telling him that he don't like it.*

I: *Does Tommy think he will be punished if he tries to make the man stop?*

A: *No.*

I: *Do you think he will be punished?*

A: *No.*

I: *What do you think will happen to Tommy?*

A: *I don't know.*

I: *Does the man care how Tommy feels? Why or why not?*

A: *No. Cause he really don't care.*

I: *Should Tommy tell anybody about what the man did? Who? Tell me everybody you can think of.*

A: *Mom and Dad, the police, that's all.*

I: *What does Tommy think will happen if he tells anybody what the man did?*

A: *The man will try to steal him.*

I: *What will the man do if Tommy tells on him?*

A: *He'll try to rob his house.*

I: *Pretend the man tells Tommy "Don't tell anybody what I did." Should Tommy keep the secret? Why or why not?*

A: *No. Cause he should tell so this guy won't keep coming up to his house and stuff.*

This older boy knows something is wrong and has a plan for responding. He spots the perpetrator's trick, as revealed by his statement that Tommy should "Tell his parents a stranger was telling him a story. . . ." However, it is interesting that his logic floats off into ideas about the stranger having actually taken a dog to accomplish the trick: Adam states "and he could have gotten in trouble for taking someone's dog." Adam suggests that Tommy may want to punch the perpetrator for touching him, yet offers that Tommy could make the stranger stop by "telling him (the stranger) that he (the boy) don't like it," a less dramatic resistance. Perhaps, in deference to adult status or stature, Adam thinks better of having Tommy actually throw a punch. Despite Adam's bravery and certainty of response, by the end of the interview fear of retribution creeps into his thinking as he states that the stranger may try to rob Tommy's house if Tommy tells on him.

Melissa, Younger Girl, Age 7 Years 10 Months, Coach Version

Interviewer: *Tell me what you think the problem is in this story.*
Melissa: *He shouldn't touch Tammy by that part, the bathing suit.*
I: *What should Tammy do? Why?*
M: *Say don't and tell.*
I: *What do you think Tammy will do? Why?*
M: *Say "Stop it and don't do that—it's uncomfortable."*
I: *The coach told Tammy to pick up the baseball bats. Should Tammy do what the coach said? Why or why not?*
M: *If she wants to, she can help, it's her job.*
I: *Was it OK for the coach to tell Tammy to pick up the baseball bats?*
M: *Yes.*
I: *Does a coach have the right to tell kids what to do? Why or why not?*
M: *Yes, if they want to be the helper.*
I: *The coach touched Tammy's bottom. What does Tammy think about that?*
M: *Tammy should think it's uncomfortable. Say "Don't do it."*
I: *Was it OK for the coach to do that?*
M: *No, because Tammy was uncomfortable.*
I: *What did Tammy want to do when the coach touched her?*
M: *No, because she really doesn't like it.*
I: *You said that Tammy should not listen to the coach. Does she have a right to disobey?*
M: *Yes.*
I: *Do kids have the right to disobey sometimes? Like when?*
M: *Yes. If she doesn't like it she doesn't have to obey.*
I: *You said it was OK for Tammy to pick up the baseball bats when the coach told her to. You said it was not OK for the coach to touch Tammy. What is the difference between those two things?*
M: *To help him is OK because it's right to do the job. Wrong to let him touch.*
I: *Is it ever OK for a kid to do what a coach tells her to do?*
M: *In her case, if she wants to be a helper, but not things bad.*
I: *Is it OK for a kid to obey any grown-up when the grown-up tells the kid to do something wrong? Why or why not?*
M: *No, should do what she thinks is right.*
I: *From what you have heard about Tammy is she a good girl?*
M: *Yes.*
I: *From what you have heard about the coach is he a good man?*
M: *Not when he touches her bottom.*

I: *Do you think Tammy and the coach get along very well?*

M: *Not when he makes her feel uncomfortable.*

I: *In this story let's pretend that the coach and Tammy do not agree about what Tammy should do. The coach wants to touch Tammy but Tammy wants the coach to stop. Can Tammy end this disagreement?*

M: *She should say stop, run away, and tell.*

I: *Why wouldn't Tammy want the coach to touch her?*

M: *It's uncomfortable for her, it's not good.*

I: *Let's say Tammy wants to make the coach stop touching her. How could she make the coach stop?*

M: *Hold his hand to make him stop, say stop, call the police.*

I: *Does Tammy think she will be punished if she tries to make the coach stop?*

M: *No, it's right for her to tell. Parents should know. Tell parents, teachers, police.*

I: *Do you think she will be punished?*

M: *No.*

I: *What do you think will happen to Tammy?*

M: *Stop and run away and tell.*

I: *What does Tammy think about the coach? Does the coach know what Tammy thinks?*

M: *She thinks he is nice but he shouldn't touch. But nobody's perfect.*

I: *Does the coach care how Tammy feels? Why or why not?*

M: *Yes. He won't stop if he doesn't care.*

I: *Should Tammy tell anybody about what the coach did? Who? Tell me everybody you can think of.*

M: *Police, kids, parents, teacher.*

I: *What does Tammy think will happen if she tells anybody what the coach did?*

M: *I don't know, but it's good to tell.*

I: *What will the coach do if Tammy tells on him?*

M: *He won't be able to hurt her if he is punished by the police or Mom and Dad.*

I: *Pretend the coach tells Tammy "Don't tell anybody what I did." Should Tammy keep the secret? Why or why not?*

M: *No. Because she could have bad dreams. It would be scary to keep it all in.*

Melissa is very knowledgeable about responding to a coach perpetrator. She said it is "uncomfortable" to be touched around the "bathing suit," references, perhaps, to previous instruction about the "private zone." She proposes her version of "Say no and go." Melissa understands assertiveness; in fact, she endorses telling on the coach, ordering him to stop, holding his hand to make him stop, and running away, all effective and powerful resistance strategies.

Melissa shows that she understands the unique features of a child's inter-action with an adult perpetrator. She distinguishes between an abusive and non-abusive situation by saying it is OK to help the coach because "it's right to do the job," but it is wrong "to let him touch." She states the coach is not a good man "when he touches her bottom," and she believes in a child's right to disobey.

At the same time, Melissa's fine social reasoning abilities reveal a vulnera-bility associated with being a child. Despite that she knows the coach touched Tammy, Melissa asserts the right to do what the coach says when a child wants to be "the helper." Late in the interview, after all Melissa's strong statements of resistance, when she is asked what Tammy thinks of the coach, this informed and assertive little girl states that "She thinks he is nice, but he shouldn't touch. *But nobody's perfect!*" Melissa believes that "if the coach cares about Tammy" he will stop touching her because Tammy wants him to. Melissa reveals the unknowns that face a child who responds to a perpetrator: She does not know what will happen to Tammy if Tammy tells. She places her confidence in the parents and police, who are charged with punishing the coach. One wonders what disappointments befall a child who reports and finds that the responses of real-world adults fall quite short of the child's fantasies of rescue. Finally, Melissa knows telling is essential because it would be "scary to keep it all in"; thus telling is needed to ward off the bad dreams that may come.

Zachary, Older Boy, Age 10 Years 6 Months, Uncle Version

> **Interviewer:** *Tell me what you think the problem is in this story.*
> **Zachary:** *He's not supposed to touch him on the bottom.*
> **I:** *What should Tommy do? Why?*
> **Z:** *He should say don't do that because it's not right.*
> **I:** *What do you think Tommy will do? Why?*
> **Z:** *He'll tell somebody. Because he doesn't like that.*
> **I:** *Uncle told Tommy to turn off the television and get ready for bed. Should Tommy do what his uncle told him to do? Why?*
> **Z:** *Yes, because his uncle told him to do that.*
> **I:** *Was it OK for his uncle to tell Tommy to do that?*
> **Z:** *Yes.*
> **I:** *Do uncles have the right to tell kids what to do?*
> **Z:** *Yes.*
> **I:** *Uncle touched Tommy's bottom. What does Tommy think about that?*
> **Z:** *He probably doesn't like it.*
> **I:** *Is it OK for his uncle to do that?*
> **Z:** *No.*
> **I:** *What did Tommy want to do when his uncle touched his bottom?*

Z: *He told him to stop it.*

I: *You said that Tommy should tell his uncle to stop it. Does he have a right to disobey his uncle?*

Z: *Yes, because he's not supposed to be doing that.*

I: *Do kids have the right to disobey sometimes? Like when?*

Z: *Sometimes, like when somebody is doing something bad to them.*

I: *You said it was OK for Tommy to listen when his uncle told him to turn off the TV and get ready for bed. You said it was not OK when his uncle touched his bottom. What is the difference between those two things?*

Z: *He's not supposed to touch his bottom and he should turn off the TV. One is wrong and one is right.*

I: *What is it about uncles that gives them the right to tell a boy what to do?*

Z: *They're like their parents. Tell them how to act if there was a fire.*

I: *Is it OK for a kid to obey any grown-up when the grown-up tells the kid to do something wrong? Why or why not?*

Z: *Not always. It could not be their parent.*

I: *From what you have heard about Tommy is he a good boy?*

Z: *Yes.*

I: *From what you have heard about the uncle is he a good man?*

Z: *No.*

I: *Do you think Tommy and his uncle get along very well?*

Z: *Yeah.*

I: *In this story let's pretend that Uncle and Tommy do not agree about what Tommy should do. Uncle wants to touch Tommy but Tommy wants him to stop. Can Tommy end this disagreement?*

Z: *Yeah.*

I: *Why wouldn't Tommy want the man to touch him?*

Z: *Because he doesn't like that.*

I: *Let's say Tommy wants to make his uncle stop touching him. How could he make him stop?*

Z: *Tell him not to do that.*

I: *Does Tommy think he will be punished if he tries to make his uncle stop?*

Z: *No.*

I: *Do you think he will be punished?*

Z: *No.*

I: *What do you think will happen to Tommy? To his uncle?*

Z: *He'd probably tell somebody. He'll probably get in trouble.*

I: *What does Tommy think about his uncle?*

Z: *He probably doesn't like him.*

I: *Does his uncle care how Tommy feels? Why or why not?*

Z: *No. Because he was doing it. He was touching his bottom.*

> **I:** *Should Tommy tell anybody about what his uncle did? Who? Tell me everybody you can think of.*
> **Z:** *Yes. The police, teacher, a grown-up friend, grandma.*
> **I:** *What does Tommy think will happen if he tells anybody what his uncle did?*
> **Z:** *He will probably get into trouble.*
> **I:** *What will his uncle do if Tommy tells on him?*
> **Z:** *He'll probably say "Why did you tell on me?"*
> **I:** *Pretend that Uncle tells Tommy "Don't tell anybody what I did." Should Tommy keep the secret? Why or why not?*
> **Z:** *No, he shouldn't, because he didn't like that.*

Zachary clearly recognizes that the uncle's actions are inappropriate, and suggests both resistance and reporting. He indicates that Tommy should direct his uncle to stop the touching and tell on the uncle. Zachary is aware that other people have their own ideas about events: He anticipates that the uncle may question Tommy with, "Why did you tell on me?"

The difficulty in defying the authority of a relative is clearly evident in Zachary's excellent attempts to reconcile his awareness that uncles should be obeyed, and yet abusive uncles are an exception. He realizes that telling a child to turn off the TV is "right" and touching is "wrong." He shows how children construct rationales regarding the limits of legitimate authority by explaining an uncle's right to be in charge when the uncle is telling a child what to do if there's a fire.

Sue, Younger Girl, Age 6 Years 4 Months, Uncle Version

> **Interviewer:** *Tell me what you think the problem is in this story.*
> **Sue:** *He shouldn't put hand on her bottom.*
> **I:** *What should Tammy do? Why?*
> **S:** *Tell Uncle to stop.*
> **I:** *What do you think Tammy will do? Why?*
> **S:** *Tell him to take his hand off fast.*
> **I:** *Uncle told Tammy to turn off the television and get ready for bed. Should Tammy do what her uncle told her to do? Why?*
> **S:** *Yes, he's the boss when mom and dad are gone.*
> **I:** *Was it OK for her uncle to tell Tammy to do that?*
> **S:** *Yes.*
> **I:** *Do uncles have the right to tell kids what to do?*
> **S:** *Yes, when parents are gone.*
> **I:** *Uncle touched Tammy's bottom. What does Tammy think about that?*
> **S:** *Scared.*

I: *Is it OK for her uncle to do that?*

S: *No.*

I: *What did Tammy want to do when her uncle touched her bottom?*

S: *Tell him to get out.*

I: *You said that Tammy should tell her uncle to stop it. Does she have a right to disobey her uncle?*

S: *Sometimes, if he does bad stuff to her.*

I: *Do kids have the right to disobey sometimes? Like when?*

S: *Yes, if something is wrong and the kid knows it's wrong.*

I: *You said it was OK for Tammy to listen when her uncle told her to turn off the TV and get ready for bed. You said it was not OK when her uncle touched her bottom. What is the difference between those two things?*

S: *He should not touch her bottom.*

I: *What is it about uncles that gives them the right to tell a girl what to do?*

S: *When they're baby-sitting them.*

I: *Is it OK for a kid to obey any grown-up when the grown-up tells the kid to do something wrong? Why or why not?*

S: *No. Won't do what's wrong.*

I: *From what you have heard about Tammy is she a good girl?*

S: *Sometimes.*

I: *From what you have heard about the uncle is he a good man?*

S: *Sometimes, not when he touches her bottom.*

I: *Do you think Tammy and her uncle get along very well?*

S: *Sometimes.*

I: *In this story let's pretend that Uncle and Tammy do not agree about what Tammy should do. Uncle wants to touch Tammy but Tammy wants him to stop. Can Tammy end this disagreement?*

S: *Yes. Say no. Stop.*

I: *Why wouldn't Tammy want Uncle to touch her?*

S: *It's not right to touch.*

I: *Let's say Tammy wants to make her uncle stop touching her. How could she make him stop?*

S: *Push him off the bed. Get her dog to get him.*

I: *Does Tammy think she will be punished if she tries to make her uncle stop?*

S: *No.*

I: *Do you think she will be punished?*

S: *Yes. Her uncle wants to do this.*

I: *What do you think will happen to Tammy? To her uncle?*

S: *She won't get in trouble. He won't come back if he does it ever again.*

I: *What does Tammy think about her uncle?*

S: *He was mean to her.*

I: *Does her uncle care how Tammy feels? Why or why not?*
S: *Yes. He'll try not to make her sad. She'll hide behind him (to protect her).*
I: *Should Tammy tell anybody about what her uncle did? Who? Tell me everybody you can think of.*
S: *Yes. Parents, grandma, uncle's father, uncle's wife.*
I: *What does Tammy think will happen if she tells anybody what her uncle did?*
S: *They'll all be mad at him.*
I: *What will her uncle do if Tammy tells on him?*
S: *He'll never do it again.*
I: *Pretend that Uncle tells Tammy "Don't tell anybody what I did." Should Tammy keep the secret? Why or why not?*
S: *No, it's important to tell, it was wrong.*

Sue is one of the youngest children in the study. Although she immediately recognizes the uncle's actions as inappropriate and suggests telling him "to take his hand off fast," she does not immediately suggest reporting. She states her awareness that kids have a right to disobey if they know something is wrong, or "if he does bad stuff to her." When she is asked who should be told of the uncle's actions, in addition to Tammy's parents and grandma, Sue suggests telling the uncle's father and wife—perhaps her idea of two authority figures who have the right to put constraints on the uncle and will "be mad at him."

Sue is a fine example of an informed and confident little girl. Still, at 6 years 4 months old, the vulnerabilities surrounding childhood reasoning are evident. Three times she maintains that the uncle is the boss "when mom and dad are gone" or when he is baby-sitting, revealing, perhaps, the young child's natural adherence to principles that govern authority relationships. Despite her confident assertions about responding to a perpetrator, she is unclear about what such an encounter means about both him and the victim. In the confusing social dilemma of encountering an abusive uncle, Sue responds in vague terms regarding the "goodness" of Tammy and her uncle. She believes Tammy may be punished for trying to make him stop. Sue believes the uncle was mean, yet affirms that he cares how Tammy feels and will "try not to make her sad" and let her "hide behind him" for protection. The betrayal of a little girl's trust in her uncle, in Sue's own words, leaves the child "scared," and her ways to protect herself are to "push him off the bed" and tell "her dog to get the uncle."

EXAMPLES OF VULNERABILITY

Ben, Younger Boy, Age 7 Years 8 Months, Stranger Version

Interviewer: *Tell me what you think the problem is in this story.*
Ben: *Tommy doesn't know the man.*

I: *What should Tommy do? Why?*

B: *Go tell his Mom and Dad to ask if he should help because the man might be lying.*

I: *What do you think Tommy will do? Why?*

B: *He'll look at the picture and see if he saw the dog.*

I: *Why?*

B: *Because he might have seen the puppy someplace and he (the dog) might be with a person he doesn't know.*

I: *The man told Tommy to look at the picture of the puppy. Should Tommy do what the man said? Why or why not?*

B: *Yes, because he could have saw him (the dog) before.*

I: *Was it OK for the man to tell Tommy to look at the picture of the dog?*

B: *Yes.*

I: *Does a man walking down the street have the right to tell kids what to do? Why or why not?*

B: *No, because it isn't their kid and only their mom and dad can tell them what to do that's fun.*

I: *The man touched Tommy's bottom. What does Tommy think about that?*

B: *I guess he shouldn't help him because he shouldn't do that— only doctors can do it because they know what they're doing and the man doesn't.*

I: *What did Tommy want to do when the man touched him?*

B: *Ignore him. Maybe just keep on playing and ignore him.*

I: *You said that Tommy should not listen to the man. Does he have a right to disobey the man?*

B: *Yes, he has a right because he should never touch him in that spot unless you're a doctor or a parent of him.*

I: *Do kids have the right to disobey sometimes? Like when?*

B: *No.*

I: *Is it ever OK for a kid to do what a man on the street tells him to do?*

B: *He really might have saw the puppy. You never touch somebody's bottom.*

I: *What is it about a grown-up like the man on the street that would give him the right to tell a kid what to do?*

B: *He thinks he's the boss or wants to be. Tommy doesn't think he is.*

I: *Is it OK for a kid to obey any grown-up when the grown-up tells the kid to do something wrong? Why or why not?*

B: *Yes, 'cause. . . .*

I: *From what you have heard about Tommy is he a good boy?*

B: *Yes, because the man was being mean and Tommy was doing what he should—he ignored him.*

I: *From what you have heard about the man is he a good man?*

B: *No, because he asked him to help him even though his puppy (may) not really be lost or he might not even have a puppy.*

I: *Do you think Tommy and the man get along very well?*

B: *No.*

I: *Why wouldn't Tommy want the man to touch him?*

B: *Because it wasn't right for him to do it.*

I: *Let's say Tommy wants to make the man stop touching him. How could he make the man stop?*

B: *Tell him to stop it. Say "If you will please stop that I will help you."*

I: *Does Tommy think he will be punished if he tries to make the man stop?*

B: *No.*

I: *Do you think he will be punished?*

B: *No, because he wants to help—he just wants him to stop (touching).*

I: *What do you think will happen to Tommy?*

B: *He'll run away with a friend or ring a doorbell of a friend's house.*

I: *What does Tommy think of the man? Does the man know what Tommy thinks?*

B: *That he shouldn't be going around asking kids to help him because he might not even have a puppy. No, because you can't read other people's minds—you can't know what they're thinking, only what you tell them out loud.*

I: *Does the man care how Tommy feels?*

B: *No, because he might not even like the man.*

I: *Should Tommy tell anybody about what the man did? Who? Tell me everybody you can think of.*

B: *Mom and Dad, neighbors, brother in college.*

I: *What does Tommy think will happen if he tells anybody what the man did?*

B: *He thinks nothing will happen because he did what he should.*

I: *What will the man do if Tommy tells on him?*

B: *Maybe look for him again and tell him "I'll keep touching you on the bottom."*

I: *Pretend the man tells Tommy "Don't tell anybody what I did." Should Tommy keep the secret? Why or why not?*

B: *No.*

Ben "almost" recognizes, resists, and reports. It is striking how the logic of the young child approaches the right answer, yet falls short of the true understanding needed to make his responses meaningful. Ben displays common features of children's reasoning about perpetrators. He wants to help find the puppy, yet he senses the stranger may be up to no good. Ben suggests that Tommy go and ask his parents if he can help the man—a variation of the childhood mandate "I gotta go ask my mom if I can." Ben knows Tommy will at least look at the picture of the dog because "he might have seen the puppy someplace."

Ben's answers show how children rely on parental authority as a blueprint for relationships. Other adults are defined as "not being parents" in terms of their right to be obeyed. Ben suggests that Tommy ignore the man and get to the important business of deciding what is really happening with the puppy. Ben says that Tommy should tell the man to stop touching him by saying "If you will please stop that I will help you." Ben believes Tommy won't be punished because Tommy has tried to help. He fears that if Tommy tells on the stranger, the stranger may return and tell him "I'll keep touching you on the bottom."

Jeff, Younger Boy, Age 8 Years 0 Months, Coach Version

> **Interviewer:** *Tell me what you think the problem is in this story.*
> **Jeff:** *No problem.*
> **I:** *What should Tommy do? Why?*
> **J:** *Kick him in the face. 'Cuz he put his hand on his bottom.*
> **I:** *What do you think Tommy will do? Why?*
> **J:** *Run away—not help him.*
> **I:** *The coach told Tommy to pick up the baseball bats. Should Tommy do what the coach said? Why or why not?*
> **J:** *Yes—because he never got to help before.*
> **I:** *Was it OK for the coach to tell Tommy to pick up the baseball bats?*
> **J:** *Yes.*
> **I:** *Does a coach have the right to tell kids what to do? Why or why not?*
> **J:** *Yes. I don't know.*
> **I:** *The coach touched Tommy's bottom. What does Tommy think about that?*
> **J:** *I don't know.*
> **I:** *Was it OK for the coach to do that?*
> **J:** *No.*
> **I:** *What did Tommy want to do when the coach touched him?*
> **J:** *Kick him in the face or punch him if he acts like a stranger.*
> **I:** *You said that Tommy should not listen to the coach. Does he have a right to disobey?*
> **J:** *Yes.*
> **I:** *Do kids have the right to disobey sometimes? Like when?*
> **J:** *Yes, like when parents are drunk.*

I: *You said it was OK for Tommy to pick up the baseball bats when the coach told him to. You said it was not OK for the coach to touch Tommy. What is the difference between those two things?*

J: *He did something bad.*

I: *Is it ever OK for a kid to do what a coach tells him to do?*

J: *Sure, all the time, he's the coach.*

I: *Is it OK for a kid to obey any grown-up when the grown-up tells the kid to do something wrong? Why or why not?*

J: *No, then they're a bad kid.*

I: *From what you have heard about Tommy is he a good boy?*

J: *Yes.*

I: *From what you have heard about the coach is he a good man?*

J: *No, he did something bad.*

I: *Do you think Tommy and the coach get along very well?*

J: *Not right now.*

I: *In this story let's pretend that the coach and Tommy do not agree about what Tommy should do. The coach wants to touch Tommy but Tommy wants the coach to stop. Can Tommy end this disagreement?*

J: *Yes, by running away.*

I: *Why wouldn't Tommy want the coach to touch him?*

J: *Cuz that's his private part.*

I: *Let's say Tommy wants to make the coach stop touching him. How could he make the coach stop?*

J: *By hitting him.*

I: *Does Tommy think he will be punished if he tries to make the coach stop?*

J: *Oh, yes, real bad.*

I: *Do you think he will be punished?*

J: *Not really, he didn't do anything bad.*

I: *What do you think will happen to Tommy?*

J: *He won't get the (helper) job and he'll be real glad.*

I: *What does Tommy think about the coach? Does the coach know what Tommy thinks?*

J: *I really don't know. I don't know.*

I: *Does the coach care how Tommy feels? Why or why not?*

J: *Probably not. Just because. I guess I don't know.*

I: *Should Tommy tell anybody about what the coach did? Who? Tell me everybody you can think of.*

J: *No! That stuff is private.*

I: *What does Tommy think will happen if he tells anybody what the coach did?*

J: *They'll laugh at him and the coach.*

I: *What will the coach do if Tommy tells on him?*

J: *I don't know.*
I: *Pretend the coach tells Tommy "Don't tell anybody what I did."*
Should Tommy keep the secret? Why or why not?
J: *Yes. Or he could tell his mom and dad 'cause they gave birth to him.*

At 8 years old, Jeff typifies the confusion a child may experience when confronted with a complex social dilemma. Jeff tries to think his answers through, but many times he says he simply does not know, as if it were all too difficult to figure out. Jeff knows something is wrong, but he is unable to construct a rationale for behaving in other than a prescribed way. His comments about not listening to parents when they are drunk suggest that he knows the experience of not relying on socially sanctioned authority figures who may tell a child to do the wrong thing.

Jeff has heard about "private parts" and recognizes the perpetrator's action as inappropriate. Yet he has limited ability to resist, and his aggressive strategies suggest a child's fantasy rather than a real plan. Jeff's responses also suggest an additional vulnerability for young children victimized by sexual abuse—a person *is* bad if he or she *does* bad. This basic feature of childhood reasoning about self and others puts children who are abused at risk for believing that they are "bad."

Sally, Younger Girl, 7 Years 6 Months, Uncle Version

Interviewer: *Tell me what you think the problem is in this story.*
Sally: *Uncle had a bad day and the niece had a good one.*
I: *What should Tammy do? Why?*
S: *If he has work to do on Saturday or Sunday she could help him to have a better day. Because her uncle had a bad day and she's having a good one that will make him have a better day.*
I: *What do you think Tammy will do? Why?*
S: *Every Saturday or Sunday, or Monday or Tuesday if she's off school she should help him.*
I: *Uncle told Tammy to turn off the television and get ready for bed. Should Tammy do what her uncle told her do? Why?*
S: *Yes, because he's like her parent.*
I: *Was it OK for her uncle to tell Tammy to do that?*
S: *Yes.*
I: *Do uncles have the right to tell kids what to do?*
S: *Yes. If a parent dies that would be the parent. Better get used to your aunt or uncle.*
I: *Uncle touched Tammy's bottom. What does Tammy think about that?*
S: *It's not really right.*

I: *Is it OK for her uncle to do that?*

S: *Yes, if he wants to.*

I: *What did Tammy want to do when her uncle touched her bottom?*

S: *Like to say "Don't do that."*

I: *You said that Tammy should tell her uncle to stop it. Does she have a right to disobey her uncle?*

S: *No, she doesn't have that right. Because he's a relative, like a parent.*

I: *Do kids have the right to disobey sometimes? Like when?*

S: *Yes, like if they tell a kid to steal.*

I: *You said it was OK for Tammy to listen when her uncle told her to turn off the TV and get ready for bed. You said it was not OK when her uncle touched her bottom. What is the difference between those two things?*

S: *Well, bottom is like privacy and TV is not.*

I: *What is it about uncles that gives them the right to tell a girl what to do?*

S: *I don't really know. They're big, you know.*

I: *Is it OK for a kid to obey any grown-up when the grown-up tells the kid to do something wrong? Why or why not?*

S: *No, because it's just the same as stealing or if they say "Kid, someone. . . ." It's just not right.*

I: *From what you have heard about Tammy is she a good girl?*

S: *Yes.*

I: *From what you have heard about the uncle is he a good man?*

S: *He's nice, and a little mean.*

I: *Do you think Tammy and her uncle get along very well?*

S: *Yes, he's her uncle.*

I: *In this story let's pretend that Uncle and Tammy do not agree about what Tammy should do. Uncle wants to touch Tammy but Tammy wants him to stop. Can Tammy end this disagreement?*

S: *Yes.*

I: *Why wouldn't Tammy want her uncle to touch her?*

S: *It's like privacy.*

I: *Let's say Tammy wants to make her uncle stop touching her. How could she make him stop?*

S: *Tell him to stop it.*

I: *Does Tammy think she will be punished if she tries to make her uncle stop?*

S: *No.*

I: *Do you think she will be punished?*

S: *No.*

I: *What do you think will happen to Tammy? To her uncle?*

S: *Her uncle will stop and she'll be happy. He'll be happy too.*

> **I:** *What does Tammy think about her uncle?*
> **S:** *She thinks he is very nice.*
> **I:** *Does her uncle care how Tammy feels? Why or why not?*
> **S:** *Yes, if he didn't care how she felt he wouldn't listen to her.*
> **I:** *Should Tammy tell anybody about what her uncle did? Who? Tell me everybody you can think of.*
> **S:** *I think she should. Her parents, cousins, the aunt, about her husband, and maybe her best friend.*
> **I:** *What does Tammy think will happen if she tells anybody what her uncle did?*
> **S:** *Nothing.*
> **I:** *What will her uncle do if Tammy tells on him?*
> **S:** *He'll get real mad.*
> **I:** *Pretend that Uncle tells Tammy "Don't tell anybody what I did." Should Tammy keep the secret? Why or why not?*
> **S:** *No, because he shouldn't have done that to her.*

Sally's responses speak volumes about the confusion of a child betrayed by a loved caregiver. She wants Tammy to attend to her uncle's bad day and make him feel better. She wants to see an uncle in a favorable light, and is reluctant to recognize, resist, and report, even as she grows in her awareness of the nature of the uncle's action. Sally's understanding of "wrong" pertains to concrete misdeeds, and she is unsure about this social situation with an uncle. Sally, like many children, wants the perpetrator to stop touching so that things can go back to the good and normal way that children need and want them to be.

WHAT CHILDREN THINK ABOUT PERPETRATORS

The Stranger

This version of the Perpetrator Interview involved a child encountering a stranger who told the child to look at a picture of his lost puppy and touched the child on the bottom. The following interview responses typify "good" responses offered by many children: They include recognition of the perpetrator's inappropriate behavior, a strategy for resistance, and an endorsement of reporting—key elements of an effective response to an abusive encounter.

> The boy is talking to a stranger, that's the problem here. (He should) go run away and tell somebody, because a stranger could be bad or good.
> If he knows karate, he should give him a good chop, pow, pow, pow. He'll tell his Mom, because a stranger has no right to touch him. Only a kid's parents and teacher can tell him what to do. (7-year-old boy)

The guy in the story is lying to the kid and the kid shouldn't believe him. He should just run away because he is not doing something right. The kid probably won't believe him (the stranger).

The kid will probably punch him and run. He should tell the man not to (touch him) or get someone older because that person could deal with him. I think the kid will probably run. He won't get anything bad done to him if the man doesn't hurt him. The kid wants the guy to go to jail. (9-year-old boy)

He could be lying to her about having a dog. She should just ask him if he is lying or not, because he might be a stranger. She should ask him real, real nice to take his hand off her bottom.

She'll want to tell because she really wants her Mommy to know. (6-year-old girl)

She doesn't know what to do. She's kind of scared. Her brain is telling her not to help him but she really wants to help him.

She should go tell her Mom and Dad that there's a guy who wants to find a lost puppy. That guy is trying to take her away. But, I think she'll help him, because everyone likes puppies.

She should tell him, "Don't touch me," and, if she was crabby, she might hit him. If she's happy, she'll just look at the picture of the dog and act like nothing is wrong when he touches her.

Yes, I guess she should tell, but whoever she tells will tell EVERYONE else and then the whole world will know—what a disaster! (10-year-old girl)

Although most victims of sexual abuse are acquainted with their molesters, parents and children continue to fear "the stranger." Findings suggest there may be good reason for these concerns. Three-fourths (75%) of the children in the Stranger group immediately recognized that a stranger who puts his hand on a child's bottom is behaving inappropriately; 25% did not. Nearly 1 in 10 did not recognize the danger of a stranger's advance even with extensive prompting.

A possible explanation for these findings may lie with the reported deception used by the stranger in the story: the search for a lost dog. Many children indicated that, even though the child in the story really should not help the stranger, the prospect of a "lost puppy" would probably result in a child taking a chance to help the dog, not the man. Assisting a needy animal is, perhaps, a more salient or familiar event for children, in comparison with the social demand of responding to a stranger's touch. It is little wonder that perpetrators use this ploy to trick children; evidence shows that, even with specific knowledge of the stranger's tactics, children could provide a rationale for why a child would comply with the stranger's request.

The Coach

The Coach version related a story of a child being selected to help the coach and the coach putting his hand on the child's bottom. Although an abusive coach is a highly recognizable perpetrator, 30% of the children did not immediately suggest resistance.

Review of individual interviews revealed that children expressed concern that a coach could kick a child off the team if the child resisted, and that parents could force the child to quit the team if a report was made to them. It appears that, for children confronted with a known perpetrator, defiance of authority may involve some weighing of costs and benefits associated with possible outcomes. Concerns about negative consequences may play a significant part in children's reactions to perpetrators. A coach not only has perceived authority, but also has perceived *power* to enact repercussions upon a child.

The following samples include responses that demonstrate recognition, resistance, and reporting of a coach perpetrator.

It's not right to touch other people. She should run away. He's not very nice and it could get worse.

He's bad. Those are special parts not meant for him. Only a parent or a doctor can touch there. Tammy would think "This might get out of control" and run.

She should listen to him, like in the game, because he's a parent figure, a teacher. So she could help with bats and stuff, but if you've heard he's bad, you shouldn't help.

She should run away and tell someone. Her parents and her school have taught her that it's bad. She could even hit or bite him. She should tell her parents, they'll question her, but not punish her.

But no more baseball for Pat. (The coach) will try to get out of it, but the police will get him. If you keep the secret it will just get worse. Tell right away and fix the problem. (9-year-old girl)

I was thinking like maybe the kid just sat down and the coach happened to put his hand there.

He could stand up and tell him to stop it, because he doesn't like the coach touching him there. But, he should listen to his coach, because a coach is in charge of the team. Just don't have to listen all of the time.

Tommy's really not too happy about this. He thought the coach really liked him, and now he sees he didn't really care. He'll tell his mom and dad. He's going to get in trouble by the coach, the coach will be mad at him. His mom and dad sure don't want strangers touching him. (10-year-old boy)

People aren't supposed to touch private parts. Tell him to leave his hands off my private parts. He should go home, he felt like he didn't want to be wanted. Like he didn't want the coach to want him for the team anymore.

He helped the coach because he thought he'd get to play probably. See, a coach doesn't have to pick up the mess, the players do.

But, see, a coach picks who is on the team. Tommy thinks he's a nice coach, but the coach doesn't care what he does to other people.

Tommy will tell his parents and they'll tell him not to go to the field anymore. Everyone will make fun of him (the coach). (7-year-old boy)

The Uncle

The present study sought to assess children's vulnerability to incest. Concerns voiced by parents and school personnel where the children were recruited precluded the inclusion of a perpetrator story depicting a father or stepfather as perpetrator. The uncle perpetrator was intended to approximate children's responses to incest overtures. The story involved an uncle telling a child to turn off the TV and go to bed, and putting his hand on the child's bottom.

Children displayed considerable vulnerability to sexual abuse by a relative. Not only did children have difficulty recognizing an uncle's actions as potentially abusive, but, even of those who did, they were unlikely to resist or report. Many children perceived an uncle as having great authority over a child because "he's like a parent when the parents are away" or "he's the one who would raise you if your parents died or something." Children believed an uncle to have an extensive range of legitimate power, including spanking if the child refused to obey. Interestingly, though an uncle's position was often cited as a rationale for obedience, children viewed an uncle as having the power to really disrupt relationships by telling a child's parents and getting the child "in trouble."

Tommy was lying if he said he had a good time with his uncle. (He should) tell his uncle not to do that, it's not good touching other people's private parts. Tommy should tell him not to do that, but he doesn't really have a right to tell adults what to do.

But turning off the TV is one thing, touching bottoms is another. One you can just get yelled at, the other is more trouble. But he's an adult and he's bigger than Tommy. It really doesn't feel comfortable.

He should tell him, "I don't want you to touch that. It doesn't feel good." I think his mom will see and say "Don't do that to my kid." He still thinks his uncle is sometimes good.

If he tells he'll get in trouble and his uncle will yell at him. It wouldn't be nice if he told anyone. (6-year-old boy)

(She should) scream. I wouldn't want my uncle to put his hand on my bottom. I'd be uncomfortable. I wouldn't kick him, but, then, my uncle wouldn't do that, I don't think.

If he'd come over again, someone should just tell him Tammy is not home, that she's at a friend's house. If I was home, I'd lock my door.

She probably felt embarrassed. She could hop out of bed and run. She shouldn't listen to her uncle when he does something wrong.

See, grown-ups can tell you what to do if you do the wrong thing, but you tell yourself (what to do) if the grown-ups do the wrong thing. She could slap him, bite him, and tell her parents. It just doesn't seem right for an uncle to do something like that.

I'd tell my mom and dad to stop having him come over. I'd tell them what he was doing to me. If that was the only time he did it, I think her parents would punish *her*. But if he was doing it all the time, then they'd believe her and she wouldn't get punished.

I think if he really kept on aggravating her, then she might not like him anymore. She should only tell her parents, because it's personal. If she told anyone else, even her friend, the whole school would know.

(If she tells) her uncle probably won't show his face anymore. But if she doesn't, he'll keep doing it. (9-year-old girl)

Tommy's uncle is putting his hand on his bottom, that's a problem. He should walk away from him, because he doesn't like that. His uncle is not his parent. An uncle can tell you what to do if he has the parents' permission.

I think Tommy will go to bed and his uncle will just sit there. He doesn't like his uncle anymore. But his uncle still loves him because he's a relative. Tommy shouldn't tell anyone except his parents and they will talk to his uncle. (10-year-old boy)

MEASURING THE QUALITY OF CHILDREN'S RESPONSES

Examination of children's own words highlights the dilemma of evaluating the actual usefulness of their ideas. Even as children explain what they know, the adult observer is left to wonder if children could effectively respond to a perpetrator. It is difficult to evaluate effective response in an interview. Yet a means of rating the ways real children respond to perpetrators needs to be developed if a truly "child-generated" model of sexual abuse intervention is to be formulated. Real children may mimic adult instructions, but they also come up with some original ways to respond to perpetrators.

ESTIMATING EFFECTIVENESS OF RESPONSE

The evaluation of resistance and reporting in the Burkhardt study involved both qualitative and quantitative measures. First, there was a straightforward counting of the number of resistance and reporting strategies a child suggested. Second, an estimated effectiveness rating for each strategy was assigned. *Effectiveness* was defined as the likelihood that a strategy would realistically stop a perpetrator.

Because there was no objective means to evaluate effectiveness, prior to conducting the Burkhardt study, an Effectiveness Research Project was designed. The question was posed: What do adults actually believe children should do to thwart a perpetrator? To investigate this question and empirically establish effectiveness ratings to be used in the Burkhardt study, data from an adult research population were collected.

Sample strategies taken from histories of actual victims of childhood sexual abuse, as well as strategies presented in child abuse prevention materials, were presented to 120 female undergraduate students. A 7-point Likert scale ranging from 1 (*highly ineffective*) to 7 (*highly effective*) was designed. The median effectiveness ratings assigned to a strategy by the undergraduate students became the value assigned by the raters in the Burkhardt study. Median effectiveness ratings appear in Table 4.1.

The effectiveness rating was a necessary supplement to evaluating children's responses. As many people who work with children know, kids often give all sorts of answers. The researcher wanted to be able to credit the children with resistance and reporting, regardless of the effectiveness of their responses. For example, if one child stated that Batman should be told about the perpetrator and another child stated that the police should be told, both were scored "Yes" for reporting because they each knew that reporting was needed. Such tallying was needed to distinguish children who knew that a response was needed from children who did not know.

Realistically, of course, there would be considerable difference between the effectiveness of reporting to Batman or to the police. Thus, the effectiveness ratings permitted a qualitative comparison of the children's abilities to resist and report. A highest effectiveness rating (HER) was assigned to the most effective strategy a child suggested, and a mean effectiveness rating (MER) was assigned by summing the effectiveness ratings for all the strategies a single child suggested and dividing by the total number of suggestions.

In this way, the children were evaluated for their best suggestions (HER) while simultaneously considering the overall quality of a child's thinking (MER). For example, a child might suggest a highly effective resistance strategy, such as "Tell him to stop touching me," but follow it with a silly suggestion such as "then call the Ninja Turtles to kill the guy." The development of the effectiveness rating system was done for investigatory purposes, and no measures of instrument reliability or validity exist.

DIFFERENCES IN CHILDREN'S RESPONSES

It was expected that the quality of the children's resistance and reporting might vary according to which version of the Perpetrator Interview they were administered. Statistical analyses provided some assistance in identifying group differences in the children's responses to perpetrators. A multivariate analysis of variance (MANOVA), with the type of perpetrator as an independent variable, was conducted to determine if there were quantitative and qualitative differences in the children's responses to a stranger, a coach, and an uncle. Quantitative response was measured by the number of resistance and reporting strategies suggested by a child (number of strategies) and the number of people a child said should be told about the perpetrator's actions (number of report targets). Qualitative response was measured by the raters' assignment for each child of an HER score and an MER score.

The results of the MANOVA test appear in Table 4.2. Significant differences among the types of perpetrators were detected [Hotellings, $F(8) = 10.74$; $p < .001$].

Table 4.1   Effectiveness Ratings

	Range	Mean	MD
Uncle			
1. Runs from bedroom to living room.	4–7	4.6	5.0
2. Tells mom.	5–7	5.6	6.0
3. Asks older brother or sister for help.	4–7	4.8	5.0
4. Hits with a fist.	1–5	3.6	3.0
5. Screams.	4–7	4.7	5.0
6. Wears extra layer of clothing to bed.	1–2	1.9	1.5
7. Pretends to be asleep.	1–3	2.5	2.0
8. Tells teacher.	5–7	5.7	6.0
9. Says directly, "Stop, don't do that."	1–5	3.9	4.0
10. Complies, but tells perpetrator, "I'll never do this again."	1–2	1.4	1.0
11. Reports perpetrator to police.	6–7	6.2	7.0
12. Tells perpetrator he or she has an upset stomach.	1–4	2.7	2.5
13. Sobs and cries.	1–4	2.9	2.0
14. Goes to live with a relative (out of the home).	5–7	5.2	6.0
15. Tucks the blankets tightly into the mattress.	1–2	1.7	1.0
16. Pretends this is happening to someone else.	1	1.2	1.0
17. Asks "P," "Why are you doing this?"	1–4	2.6	2.0
18. Tells favorite aunt about "P's" behavior.	3–7	4.4	5.0
19. Threatens to tell mom.	1–5	3.0	3.0
Coach			
1. Runs away.	5–7	5.8	6.0
2. Tells mom.	6–7	6.3	7.0
3. Asks older boy or girl in the park for help.	3–6	4.5	5.0
4. Hits with a fist.	1–4	3.4	3.0
5. Screams.	4–7	4.5	5.0
6. Tells coach he or she has to go home for supper.	1–2	2.4	2.0
7. Pretends not to hear what Coach said.	1–3	2.4	2.0
8. Tells teacher.	5–7	6.0	2.0
9. Says directly, "Stop, don't do that."	3–7	4.7	5.0
10. Complies, but tells perpetrator, "I'll never do this again."	1	1.2	1.0

(Continued)

Subsequent univariate analyses revealed significant group differences in all of the qualitative and quantitative measures of response. These findings show that the type of perpetrator presented to the children affected the way in which they were able to respond in terms of the number of resistance and reporting strategies they suggested, the number of report targets they mentioned, and the effectiveness of the strategies they proposed.

Number of Resistance and Reporting Strategies

On the average, children in the Uncle group offered 2.15 strategies for resisting and reporting an uncle (Table 4.2). This number was significantly less than the

Table 4.1 Effectiveness Ratings *(Continued)*

	Range	Mean	MD
11. Reports perpetrator to police.	6–7	6.3	7.0
12. Tells perpetrator he or she has an upset stomach.	1–4	2.4	2.0
13. Sobs and cries.	1–4	2.7	3.0
14. Quits team.	1–3	2.6	2.0
15. Steps out of the little room.	4–7	5.0	5.0
16. Pretends this is happening to someone else.	1	1.4	1.0
17. Asks "P," "Why are you doing this?"	1–4	2.6	2.0
18. Tells favorite aunt about "P's" behavior.	1–7	3.4	3.0
19. Tells Coach he or she is going to tell h—parents.	1–7	4.2	5.0
Stranger			
1. Runs away.	5–7	5.9	6.0
2. Tells mom.	4–7	5.2	6.0
3. Asks older boy or girl on the street for help.	3–7	5.0	5.0
4. Hits with a fist.	1–4	3.0	2.0
5. Screams.	4–7	5.5	6.0
6. Tells perpetrator he or she has to be home for supper.	1–4	2.2	2.0
7. Pretends he or she did not hear what perpetrator said.	1–5	2.8	2.0
8. Tells teacher.	5–7	5.9	6.0
9. Says directly, "Stop, don't do that."	4–7	4.8	5.0
10. Complies, but tells perpetrator, "I'll never do this again."	1	1.0	1.0
11. Reports perpetrator to police.	6–7	6.5	7.0
12. Tells perpetrator he or she has an upset stomach.	1–2	1.9	1.0
13. Sobs and cries.	1–3	2.4	2.0
14. Stays in the house.			4.5
15. Backs away from the man.	1–7	4.2	4.0
16. Pretends this is happening to someone else.	1	1.2	1.0
17. Asks "P," "Why are you doing this?"	1–4	2.4	2.0
18. Tells favorite aunt about "P's" behavior.	4–7	5.5	6.0
19. Tells perpetrator he or she is going to tell parents.	4–7	4.7	5.0

Note. These resistance and reporting strategies were presented to undergraduate students for effectiveness rating. The median (MD) reflects the rating at the midpoint of the actual scores assigned to raters.

averages for both the Stranger (mean = 3.0) and Coach (mean = 2.9) groups. No difference between the Stranger and Coach groups was demonstrated.

Number of Report Targets

Children in the Uncle group identified fewer people to be told about an abusive uncle (mean = 1.5) in comparison with the average number of people to be told about a stranger perpetrator (mean = 2.78) or a coach perpetrator (mean = 2.2; Table 4.2). No difference between the Stranger and Coach groups was demonstrated.

Highest Effectiveness Ratings

The HER estimated each child's best plan for halting a perpetrator. The ratings of the best plans offered by children in the Uncle group (mean = 4.8) were

Table 4.2   Measures of Quality of Response to Perpetrators

A. Multivariate Analyses (Hotellings)

Effect	DF	F	p
Type of perpetrator	8	10.74	.001
Age	4	6.45	.001
Sex	4	.47	.761
Perpetrator x age	8	1.52	.154
Perpetrator x sex	8	2.28	.023
Age x sex	4	1.74	.148
Perp x age x sex	8	1.01	.425

B. Number of Resistance and Reporting Strategies: Group Means

Group	Mean	SD
Perpetrator Conditions		
Stranger (N = 37)	3.00	0.88
Coach (N = 39)	2.95	0.82
Uncle (N = 39)	2.15	0.37
Age Conditions		
Younger (N = 56)	2.29	1.04
Older (N = 59)	3.08	1.01
Sex Conditions		
Girls (N = 56)	2.79	1.17
Boys (N = 59)	2.61	1.07
Perpetrator Conditions by Age		
Stranger		
Younger (N = 18)	2.72	0.75
Older (N = 19)	3.26	0.93
Coach		
Younger (N = 19)	2.58	0.69
Older (N = 20)	3.30	0.80
Uncle		
Younger (N = 19)	1.58	1.22
Older (N = 20)	2.70	1.30

(Continued)

significantly lower than the ratings for the best plans offered by the children in the Stranger (mean = 6.8) and the Coach (mean = 6.7) groups (Table 4.2). No difference between the Stranger and Coach groups was demonstrated.

Mean Effectiveness Ratings

The MER estimated the overall quality of a child's resistance and reporting strategies by averaging the ratings of all proposed strategies. (In this way, silly

Table 4.2   Measures of Quality of Response to Perpetrators
(Continued)

C. Highest and Mean Effectiveness Ratings: Group Means		
Group	**Mean**	*SD*
Perpetrator Conditions		
Stranger (*N* = 37)		
High	6.76	0.50
Mean	5.47	0.82
Coach (*N* = 39)		
High	6.74	0.64
Mean	5.55	0.68
Uncle (*N* = 39)		
High	4.82	1.95
Mean	3.86	1.43
Age Conditions		
Younger (*N* = 56)		
High	5.71	1.82
Mean	4.84	1.53
Older (*N* = 59)		
High	6.48	1.07
Mean	5.05	1.01
Sex Conditions		
Girls (*N* = 56)		
High	6.23	1.46
Mean	5.05	1.27
Boys (*N* = 59)		
High	5.97	1.58
Mean	4.86	1.31
Perpetrator Conditions by Age		
Stranger		
Younger (*N* = 18)		
High	6.61	0.61
Mean	5.54	0.85
Older (*N* = 19)		
High	6.89	0.32
Mean	5.40	0.80
Coach		
Younger (*N* = 19)		
High	6.63	0.76
Mean	5.59	0.84
Older (*N* = 20)		
High	6.85	0.49
Mean	5.51	0.51
Uncle		
Younger (*N* = 19)		
High	3.95	2.04
Mean	3.43	1.60
Older (*N* = 20)		
High	5.65	1.46
Mean	4.27	1.13

(Continued)

Table 4.2   Measures of Quality of Response to Perpetrators
(Continued)

Group	Mean	SD
D. Number of Report Targets: Group Means		
Perpetrator Conditions		
Stranger (*N* = 37)	2.68	1.96
Coach (*N* = 39)	2.21	1.40
Uncle (*N* = 39)	1.51	1.54
Age Conditions		
Younger (*N* = 56)	1.61	1.74
Older (*N* = 59)	2.61	1.51
Sex Conditions		
Girls (*N* = 56)	2.14	1.51
Boys (*N* = 59)	2.10	1.87
Perpetrator Conditions by Age		
Stranger		
Younger (*N* = 18)	2.22	2.18
Older (*N* = 19)	3.11	1.66
Coach		
Younger (*N* = 19)	1.89	1.37
Older (*N* = 20)	2.50	1.40
Uncle		
Younger (*N* = 19)	0.74	1.28
Older (*N* = 20)	2.25	1.41
Perpetrator Conditions by Sex		
Stranger		
Girls (*N* = 18)	1.94	1.47
Boys (*N* = 19)	3.37	2.14
Coach		
Girls (*N* = 19)	2.84	1.34
Boys (*N* = 20)	1.60	1.49
Uncle		
Girls (*N* = 19)	1.63	1.50
Boys (*N* = 20)	1.40	1.60

or outrageous suggestions would lower the MER even if highly effective strategies also had been suggested.) Again, children administered the Uncle version of the Perpetrator Interview averaged MER scores of 3.86, significantly lower than the MER scores of children in the Stranger (mean = 5.47) and Coach (mean = 5.55) groups (Table 4.2). No difference between the Stranger and Coach groups was demonstrated.

AGE GROUP COMPARISONS IN QUALITY OF RESPONDING

Older children generated more strategies, suggested more effective strategies, and identified more report targets than the younger children. A summary of the average response scores appears in Table 4.2.

DIFFERENCES BETWEEN BOYS' AND GIRLS' QUALITY OF RESPONDING

In general, no significant differences between boys' and girls' scores in terms of the quality and quantity of resistance and reporting were in evidence. However, an unexpected interaction between sex and the type of perpetrator was detected. Boys in the Coach group named significantly fewer people to be told about a perpetrator than girls in the Coach group. Boys did not want to report a coach because they were concerned about being removed from the team or benched from play by the offender.

CHILD-GENERATED RESPONSES

The Burkhardt study demonstrated that vulnerability to childhood sexual abuse may be a function of children's developing social reasoning capabilities. Developing, but not fully developed, social reasoning is a part of childhood. A child-generated model of prevention and treatment of childhood sexual abuse incorporates the strengths, weaknesses, pitfalls, perils, and pearls of wisdom that originate from the children.

SUMMARY

Chapter 4 reported the findings of the Burkhardt study in terms of how children respond to perpetrators. Group comparisons suggest that children confronting a related perpetrator are at greater risk for failure to respond than children facing an unrelated perpetrator. Older girls emerged as the group most likely to recognize a perpetrator. Younger boys were especially vulnerable, with low rates of recognition, resistance, and reporting compared with other groups. Older children, as predicted, demonstrated less vulnerability than younger children.

Certain features of childhood vulnerability to sexual abuse are difficult to quantify. Excerpts from the children's responses relate uncertainty, confusion, and inadequacy in terms of their ability to generate reasons for not obeying an adult, even an abusive one, and what to do if an inappropriate encounter occurs. The children's own words offer the promise of devising a child-generated model of treatment and prevention that builds on their natural understanding of adults, including perpetrators.

A Child-Generated Model of Sexual Abuse Intervention

A child-generated model of sexual abuse intervention promotes prevention and treatment based on an understanding of normal childhood reasoning about adults, in general, and perpetrators, in particular. To date, developmental factors have been overlooked or minimized in formulations of vulnerability to childhood sexual abuse. During childhood, compliance with authority and appeasement of adults represent the attainment of social reasoning and adaptive behavior (Damon, 1977; Selman, 1980). Perpetrators may exploit this aspect of normal childhood development. A child-generated model of sexual abuse intervention supports using the characteristics of children's reasoning to develop realistic ways to protect children and heal victims.

The normal limits of children's social awareness put them at risk for being confused by perpetrators and unable to effectively respond. The Burkhardt study identified two primary factors of developmental vulnerability to childhood sexual abuse: (a) the characteristics of children's social reasoning, and (b) children's repertoire of responses to a perpetrator. The findings of the Burkhardt study suggest six principles of a child-generated model of sexual abuse intervention:

1 Children experience predictable changes in social reasoning about adults, including perpetrators.
2 Vulnerability to childhood sexual abuse is, in part, a function of children's social reasoning about adults.

3 All children are at risk for inadequate response in an encounter with a perpetrator.

4 Vulnerability to childhood sexual abuse may be greatest with a related perpetrator.

5 Protecting children is the responsibility of concerned adults because there are limits to children's abilities to protect themselves.

6 When children respond to a perpetrator, they expect their efforts to be effective.

LISTENING TO CHILDREN

Simple things can be puzzling for children. Why must I do what my teacher says? Why does my mom or dad punish me for not cleaning my room? Children author answers to such questions, and their answers are based on the reasoning they possess at a certain age and developmental stage. Their reasons may not meet adult standards of logic, common sense, or safety. Yet child after child passes through phases in which he or she thinks and talks and understands in the same "limited" ways as his or her peers.

Developmental researchers join the ranks of parents and teachers in discovering the interesting, incredible ways in which children think, the limitations to what they understand, and the innocence, confusion, naivety, and openness with which they confront life's social mysteries. Studies such as those of Damon (1977), Selman (1980), and Bruss-Saunders (1979) tracked the acquisition of social reasoning and provided valuable descriptions of what is typical.

Children are often told what to think and do. Yet children now, as always, continue to craft uniquely "childish" rationales for understanding what people do. They rely on their subjective understanding to guide their responses in social situations.

Thus, it is possible to anticipate how children may respond in social situations, even abusive ones, because they develop social reasoning about adults and authority in a predictable manner. Their thoughts affect their actions, and their words reveal their understanding.

CHARACTERISTICS OF CHILDREN'S REASONING ABOUT PERPETRATORS

Many children in the Burkhardt study gave responses that revealed their belief in a perpetrator's authority. The following examples demonstrate the progression of social reasoning from an unquestioning belief in the perpetrator's right to obedience to the "situation-specific" obedience associated with more advanced social cognition.

Does that man have the right to tell kids what to do?

"Yes." (6-year-old girl, uncle)
"Yes." (6-year-old boy, coach)

"Yes, he's the grown-up." (6-year-old boy, coach)

"Yes, he's an adult." (10-year-old girl, uncle)

"No, because he's not a real parent." (9-year-old boy, coach)

"Depends on what it is." (9-year-old girl, stranger)

"I don't know." (7-year-old boy, uncle)

"Well, just only about the game, like to teach kids about the game and help them learn the game." (9-year-old boy, coach)

"If the whole team's going to learn something, but if he's just bossing people around—no." (10-year-old girl, coach)

In response to the Perpetrator Interview, the children demonstrated the following characteristics in regards to perpetrators:

1 Many children overlook, rationalize, or deny inappropriate adult behavior, especially that of a trusted adult.

2 Children respond to sexually inappropriate actions by wanting to resist and report the perpetrator.

3 Children rely on physically fleeing the perpetrator as a means to resist and telling their parents as a means to report.

4 Children do not demonstrate a real understanding of why a perpetrator should not touch them.

5 Even as they endorse resisting and reporting a perpetrator, children develop concerns about the consequences of these actions.

6 Children specifically fear the social consequences of resisting and reporting a perpetrator.

7 Children may believe that related perpetrators are entitled to obedience.

8 Many children hope to continue a positive relationship with a known perpetrator after resisting and reporting occur.

9 Children can distinguish between abusive and nonabusive social situations with adults, and between legitimate and illegitimate uses of authority.

10 Children agree to keep secrets to avoid conflict.

11 Children are better at recognizing and reporting perpetrators than they are at thinking of ways to resist.

CHILD-GENERATED PREVENTION OF CHILDHOOD SEXUAL ABUSE

Prevention programs should build on children's natural reasoning abilities in teaching responses to perpetrators. Social reasoning characteristics should be incorporated into prevention efforts in the following ways.

Child-Generated Strategies

What should the child do?

"When she leaves, tell someone older. They would tell you what to do." (9-year-old girl)

"Leave, because the man is being mean." (6-year-old boy)

"He can just say no and if his uncle is nice he won't do it anymore." (10-year-old boy)

The inclusion of child-generated strategies for recognizing, resisting, and reporting perpetrators promotes prevention education by increasing the likelihood that students will understand, remember, and utilize what they are taught. Using the words and ideas of other children may more readily engage students in the prevention curriculum. Guided role plays and media presentations with scripts that match how children really think and talk better prepare children to respond to dangerous social situations. These findings corroborate the prevention education outcome studies that demonstrate that programs including student participation are more effective than passive educational programs (Finkelhor & Strapko, 1992; Wurtele & Miller-Perrin, 1992).

Focus on Social Features of Perpetrator

Tell me what you think the problem is in this story.

"Pat was doing something for the coach and the coach was really liking her." (10-year-old girl)

"Her uncle shouldn't be touching her." (9-year-old girl)

"It's not good to do stuff to Tammy, like kiss and stuff." (10-year-old girl)

"Yeah, there's a problem, why would he be carrying the equipment—oh, and he touched his bottom, too." (6-year-old boy)

"Touching her in the wrong place." (9-year-old girl)

"The dog is lost." (6-year-old boy)

"The man might try to trick him and take him away from his parents and kill him." (7-year-old boy)

Social cognition occurs as an interaction between an individual and his or her social environment. Therefore, prevention programs that stress what happens in a social encounter with an adult authority figure provide children an opportunity to expand their social awareness. The unique social demands of an abusive encounter should be emphasized, including situational cues that distinguish appropriate from inappropriate adult requests, rationales for disobedience, and strategies for confronting the fear and uncertainty associated with reporting.

Provide Children with Rationales for Obedience and Disobedience

Children know that they do not have to obey when an adult tells them to do something wrong. Using normal aspects of social reasoning, such as the tendency to construct rationales for obedience and disobedience, can serve to prepare children for responding to perpetrators.

You said it was OK for (the child) to obey when Uncle said to turn off the TV. You said it was not OK when Uncle touched the child's bottom. What is the difference between those things?

"TV wasn't a bad thing. Touching her is wrong." (10- year-old girl)

"It's OK to do what you're told if it's right. Not OK to do it if it's wrong." (7-year-old boy)

"Turning off the TV and going to bed is right. Tommy's uncle touching him is not right." (10-year-old boy)

"One's badder than the other. When the man touched is badder." (6-year-old boy)

Do kids have the right to disobey sometimes?

"When a stranger comes up to you." (7-year-old boy)

"Sometimes, when someone tells you to do something wrong." (9-year-old girl)

"Yes, when people are doing something bad like hitting them or touching them."

'Yes, when a mom says don't listen to them." (6-year-old girl)

Adult-generated instruction often attempts to avoid laying blame, causing guilt, or creating "dirty" feelings about sex by not labeling sexual activity between a child and an adult as *wrong*. Yet children understand that *wrong* means something they should not do, even when they do not understand why. Without a powerful and clear concept like *wrong*, children may not understand why they have a right to disobey a perpetrator.

Children are informed of "good touch" and "bad touch," of comfortable and uncomfortable feelings—concepts that may be vague and confusing. Many children in the Burkhardt study indicated that the main character wanted the perpetrator to stop touching because the touching made the child feel bad or uncomfortable. What if real touching does not make the child feel "bad," but rather makes the child feel a new, exciting, unexplained type of "good"? Children looking for "bad" to signal danger may be better served by looking for "wrong" to set the protective reflexes in motion.

Some children did not understand the touching, but believed something wrong was happening. Some children clearly identified "bad" touch and how it might make a child feel.

What does the child think about the man touching?

"That he is going to spank him." (7-year-old boy)

"She might get dirt on her." (6-year-old girl)

"She would feel mad and uncomfortable." (9-year-old girl)

"Well, you see, that's not such a good idea." (7-year-old boy)
"It's just not right." (10-year-old boy)

How can children be told that sexual abuse is wrong without being told that touch, sex, arousal, and their bodies are bad? Children understand the concept of *rules*, which should be followed regardless of whether they feel like it or whether they agree with the rule. It may be useful to instruct children that there are rules about touching that children are expected to learn and follow, that adults who break the rules should be reported, and that children can count on approval for following the rules and for telling on those who do not.

Perpetrators with varying degrees of authority may trigger different rationales for resistance and reporting. A rationale such as "I don't have to listen to him because he's not my father" readily empowers a child to disobey a stranger. In the case of a related perpetrator, a rationale based on "I don't have to listen to any adult, even my parents, if they tell me to do something wrong" may be very sensible to a child.

Present Children with Realistic Strategies

"She can ask him real, real nice, 'Please take your hand off my bottom.'" (6-year-old girl)
"Ask him to stop touching him." (10-year-old boy)
"Run away." (6-year-old boy)
"Run over by his parents." (9-year-old boy)

Blatant assertiveness toward a perpetrator and orderly resistance and reporting efforts may be contrary to the normal developmental press to obey legitimate authority. Although the prevention literature frequently touts assertiveness as a means to rebuff a perpetrator, such social behavior seems incompatible with normal social development in school-age children. "Good" children try to obey adults. In rebuffing a perpetrator, parents and teachers are prompting children to respond to an exception to a social rule. Even if children are able to recognize the need to disobey, they are likely to struggle with finding a way to do so. Prevention programs should supply realistic strategies that are as effective as possible.

Include Strategies for Responding to Related Perpetrators

What did the child want do when Uncle touched his or her bottom?

"Call up her mother and tell her." (7-year-old boy)
"Say 'Stop.'" (8-year-old boy)
"Hop out of bed and run." (9-year-old girl)

"Tell her parents 'cuz he was rude." (8-year-old girl)
"I really don't know." (6-year-old girl)

Children and parents have great difficulty knowing how to respond to a related perpetrator. Resisting and reporting of an uncle were consistently found to be less likely than responding to other perpetrators. The most effective responses included asking the relative to stop touching and reporting the relative to a parent. Saying "no" and leaving also remain good advice for children.

Include Parent Education

What will happen if the child tells?

"The parents will handle it." (9-year-old girl)
"They won't let him baby-sit anymore." (9-year-old girl)
"Parents will say, 'Son, he shouldn't have done it.'" (7-year-old boy)

Educating parents about protecting their children, including how to respond to a child's report of a perpetrator, is an important feature of prevention. Findings suggest that, given their limited ability to protect themselves in complicated social situations, children rely on parents to intervene on their behalf. Children should not be blamed for failing to protect themselves. They should not be demeaned for the ineffectiveness, the naivete, or the "unreasonableness" of the solutions they attempt. Cognitive maturation, like biological maturation, takes time. Concerned adults can provide help by patiently listening, gently questioning, and carefully clarifying the social dilemmas their children experience.

The limitations of children's social reasoning should alert concerned adults of the real risks that accompany normal development. Adults would not entrust a young child with a $100 bill and expect him or her, with undeveloped mathematical capabilities, to transact a purchase and secure the correct amount of change. Yet adults may charge children with the responsibility of providing for their own emotional well-being and physical safety, armed simply with the admonishment, "Be careful. Don't talk to strangers." As parents and educators strive to arm children with the ability to resist and report sexual abuse perpetrators, those adults would do well to remember that normal, healthy children count on grown-ups to protect and guide them through life's confusing moments.

HOW CHILDREN FAIL TO RECOGNIZE PERPETRATORS

"Tommy shouldn't listen to the man. 'Cuz he don't know if the man is a stranger." (7-year-old boy)
"His uncle wants to talk to him 'cuz he's the favorite." (10-year-old boy)
"She should just forget about it and go to sleep." (7-year-old girl)

"He could be lying about the dog. Tell him if lying or not." (6-year-old girl)

"Tammy might see the dog out her window and give it to the man." (6-year-old girl)

Average children do not think and reason like adults, nor do they think and reason as adults *tell* them to. Rather, children's thinking and reasoning abilities unfold over time and experience (Inhelder & Piaget, 1958). The children of the Burkhardt study demonstrated that responding to a perpetrator is not only associated with social reasoning, but also with the complexity of the social reasoning task. Knowing how to recognize, resist, and report an uncle is more difficult for a child to understand than responding to a stranger or a coach.

Flavell's (1985) steps for social cognition provide a framework for understanding why children may not recognize abusive actions. First, they may not know of the existence of sexually toned encounters with adults. Children cannot understand or assimilate such an interaction because they have no existing knowledge or experience. A naive child approached by a perpetrator for the first time may literally have no ideas about what to do. No doubt many young children are vulnerable at this level.

Even children who have been taught about the possibility of perpetrators may not realize the significance of a perpetrator's actions at the time of the interaction. Perpetrators seldom announce, "I'm here to touch your private parts." Rather, it seems perpetrators often deliberately disguise the nature and purpose of their actions because they already know what prevention programs are discovering: Children, no matter how often they are warned, are easily confused and distracted. In summary, it seems children are at risk for not recognizing that a perpetrator is behaving inappropriately when: (a) they are unaware of the existence of sexual abuse, or (b) they have been misled or tricked into not attending to the perpetrator's actions.

IMPROVING RECOGNITION

"He shouldn't have done that 'cause that's a private part." (6-year-old girl)

"People aren't suppose to touch other private parts." (7-year-old boy)

"The problem is that the coach shouldn't do that because that's sort of like child abuse—and the kid could get very scared." (9-year-old boy)

"Her uncle loves her—but wrong. She should run away because he loves her very much." (6-year-old girl)

In general, programs that teach children about sexual abuse and instruct them in how to respond to perpetrators reduce vulnerability (Bogat & McGrath, 1993; Hazzard et al., 1991; Tutty, 1994; Wurtele & Miller-Perrin, 1992). The limitations of these programs, in terms of offering children real protection, have also been presented (Budin & Johnson, 1989; Daro, 1991; Green, 1993; Madak &

Berg, 1992; Pelcovitz et al., 1992). A child-generated model of sexual abuse intervention calls for the addition of stories and scripts that use the words and ideas of children the same ages as the children being instructed. Instruction should begin with the children describing and discussing, in detail, their understanding of the social situations surrounding abuse, with educational efforts building on their existing knowledge and level of social reasoning.

HOW CHILDREN RESIST

What should the child do?

"Ask uncle to stop and move away. He doesn't have a right to touch her." (10-year-old girl)

"Tell the coach to pick another kid." (9-year-old boy)

"Tell him to cut it out." (9-year-old boy)

"Say 'I don't really want to do this. Pick somebody else (to pick up bats).' " (6-year-old girl)

"Try to get away." (6-year-old girl)

"Turn over and pretend to be asleep so his uncle will just go downstairs and watch TV." (10-year-old boy)

"She could scream and kick him (uncle)." (9-year-old girl)

"Tell him to leave his own hands off my private parts." (7-year-old boy)

"Hit him with a bat and run." (9-year-old boy)

"I have no idea." (9-year-old boy)

"I don't know, leave the room or something." (9-year-old boy)

Many children in the study offered sound resistance and reporting strategies. They endorsed telling parents, they explained that "bad touch" was not to be kept a secret if the perpetrator was to be stopped, and they wanted to flee or avoid the perpetrator. Yet the children's ambivalence about enacting these responses was evident. They expressed concern about embarrassing or punitive social consequences of resisting, and loss of emotional ties with perpetrators or family. Given the realistic nature of these fears, it is understandable that at least some children would not want to resist, particularly if they thought that the perpetrator's actions weren't "too bad."

IMPROVING RESISTANCE

What do you think the child will do?

"Run away, so he doesn't get hurt." (7-year-old boy)

"I think maybe yell, or do something to him, like pinch or something." (6-year-old girl)

"Walk away from him because he doesn't like what he's doing." (10-year-old boy)

"He should say no and run, say 'Stop it.'" (9-year-old boy)

What will happen to the child if he or she tries to make him stop?

"Nothing. It's her right to complain." (10-year-old girl)

Returning again to Flavell's framework for an act of social cognition, resistance requires a child to realize the need for a social response and have a repertoire of responses available. Thus, once a child recognizes the social significance of a perpetrator's actions, the child needs to know what to do.

Teaching resistance strategies is essential for reducing vulnerability to sexual abuse. However, what children are told to do must be realistic, effective, and performable by a child. Because adults may not know exactly what responses actually work, it is little wonder that the children do not know. Offenders indicate that a child's initial resistance is a powerful deterrent to abuse. The effectiveness ratings generated by female undergraduate students show what some adults believe about resisting and reporting perpetrators. Additional research can help clarify this important aspect of sexual abuse prevention.

WHY CHILDREN DON'T TELL

What will happen if he or she tells anybody what the man did?

"The man will hit him." (7-year-old boy)

"He'll threaten to hurt her parents or sister." (10-year-old girl)

"The coach will kick him off the team." (9-year-old boy)

"The coach will get really made at him." (9-year-old boy)

"She will get in serious trouble." (6-year-old girl)

"I think she'll get in trouble." (6-year-old girl)

"Her uncle will punish her." (6-year-old girl)

"Her uncle will try to get blamed, like deny it." (9-year-old girl)

"Tommy shouldn't tell. His parents will tell him not to go to the field anymore." (7-year-old boy)

"Everybody would all start making fun of him." (7-year-old boy)

"Coach will say, 'You better not (tell) or I'll hurt you.'" (9-year-old boy)

"All the kids will laugh at her." (6-year-old girl)

"Tommy will get hollered at. The coach will hit him." (7-year-old boy)

The children's most frequently cited reasons for not reporting a perpetrator revolved around negative consequences: fear of getting in trouble, worry about being denied privileges or favors, concern about being laughed at or physically hurt, not being believed, or fear of retaliation by the perpetrator.

The older boys in the study explained their concerns about reporting in terms of what others might think about them for reporting a sexual advance from another male. Many children did not want to report the stranger because they assessed that, by the time the main character got home, the incident with the stranger was over. With no continued threat present, many children saw no need to report; the main character had "handled" the situation, and might be "yelled at" by a parent for having talked with the strange man in the first place. Only if the stranger returned, or if there was a possibility of catching him, did the older children believe in reporting to parents.

The reasons for not reporting a coach had to do with the fear of being removed from the team by protective parents who would no longer allow the child to play on the coach's team. Again, many older children considered the situation solved if the main character got away from the coach and planned to avoid him in the future.

Reporting an uncle was a problematic situation for most children. The children feared repercussions from parents, relatives, and the uncle. One girl stated, "Well, she should tell on him, but her uncle won't get her no more nice Christmas presents anymore." Fear that parents would not believe a child was common, with the child concerned that the uncle would deny what he did and the child would be accused of making up a lie about "your nice, nice uncle."

The children struggled to understand how to report. One girl asked whether the uncle was the mom's brother or the dad's brother because one might want to tell the unrelated parent first. Most children expressed some worry about encountering the perpetrator in the future, after reporting, and being uncomfortable with facing him.

WHO CHILDREN WANT TO TELL

"Her parents, and grandma and grandpa." (6-year-old girl)

"His parents, grandparents, aunts and uncle." (7-year-old boy)

"The only person that she should tell is her mom and dad." (6-year-old girl)

"He's gonna tell his parents what happened and his parents will say, 'Are you OK?' " (9-year-old boy)

"His parents, and the police." (10-year-old girl)

"Only his parents, 'cuz it's personal." (9-year-old girl)

"Police, firemen, parents, and neighbors." (8-year-old boy)

" . . . the whole army." (6-year-old boy)

Parents and relatives, particularly grandparents, were the most frequently identified report targets. Many children expressed a belief that parents would "know how to handle" the perpetrator. Children who endorsed reporting wanted to tell someone they perceived as powerful, not merely trustworthy.

Children wanted to report to someone who was in a position of strength: someone forceful and protective who could influence, control, contain, or punish the perpetrator. Some children wanted vindication, and some wanted revenge. The children responded that the main character should report the incident to parents, grandparents, police, even "the whole army." Many children endorsed reporting the perpetrator so that "they can get him."

The children often expressed their sincere belief that these figures would bring the perpetrator to swift justice and provide protection from any harm or retaliation by the perpetrator. These findings suggest that children at least believe that the first goal of reporting is to tell an adult who has the power to do something about the perpetrator. Other children feared hurting the perpetrator's feelings, and did not want to tell anyone because the perpetrator might not like the main character anymore.

Adults may think that children want to confide in a caring, kind, trustworthy person; in fact, the children in the study overwhelmingly preferred strong authority figures who were perceived as empowered to protect. Police were the second most frequently named category of report targets. The fact that several children mentioned firemen as appropriate parties suggests that adults with high profiles for strength, protection, courage, and availability are the people that kids value most when they think about reporting.

Surprisingly, teachers were mentioned by only 9 of the 115 children (8%) as people to whom a report could be made. Although most of the children in the study had received some form of sexual abuse prevention education as part of their curriculum, teachers, school counselors, and other accessible adults were not mentioned. Abrahams et al. (1992) found, in their survey of 568 teachers, that a majority of teachers acknowledge confronting all types of child abuse in the classroom and feel they have insufficient education on how to address it. Teachers, as a group, may not be adults to whom children choose to report sexual abuse.

IMPROVING REPORTING

"He probably should tell his mom. I guess she'd want to know." (9-year-old boy)

"His parents will have a real talk with his uncle." (10-year-old boy)

What do you think will happen to the child if he or she tells?

"He probably won't get scolded. He will be rewarded by his parents." (7-year-old boy)

"Tell mom and dad. They will settle it." (9-year-old girl)

"They'll blame her uncle and not her. Parents will thank her for telling them. Uncle will get punished." (9-year-old girl)

Should the child keep it a secret?

"No, because if he doesn't tell someone he'll do it to somebody else." (7-year-old boy)

"She should tell him she will keep the secret until he leaves, then tell her mom and dad." (9-year-old girl)

It seems that some children harbor fantasies of being heroes if they report. Minimally, they want some acknowledgment and praise for the supreme effort it takes to report. Prevention programs and parents might influence reporting behavior by promising to praise or reward children for "telling."

THE TRAGEDY OF INCEST

Incest involves the sexual abuse of a child by a family member, often a father or stepfather. Children frequently discredited a perpetrator's authority by using this rationale: You don't have to listen to him. He's not your parent. Parental authority appeared to be the standard against which other authority relationships were measured. Extrapolation of the findings of this study to incest suggests that children confronted with an abusive relative would find it difficult to reason about legitimacy and authority.

Many average children may be unable to formulate a rationale for disobeying a parent. Given the significant amount of faith that children place in their parents' protective abilities, it is quite likely that incest overtures lead a child to feel helpless, trapped, and unempowered.

Children know they should obey their parents, even when the children do not obey. Children believe their parents should know best, even when the children do not like what their parents say. Vulnerability to incest represents a cruel misuse of the normal social developmental accomplishment of childhood. As demonstrated in the following excerpts, good, healthy, normal children create rationales for doing what their trusted adults tell them to do, even when they do not understand, even when it hurts, and even if they suspect that what they are told to do may be wrong.

What is the problem in this story?

"There's no problem here. Tommy should go to sleep because it's bedtime. His uncle can tell him what to do because he's an adult."

What does Tommy think about the touching?

"I don't know."

Was it OK for his uncle to do that?

"Yes."

What did Tommy want to do when his uncle touched his bottom?

"Do it back to him."

Why wouldn't Tommy want his uncle to touch him?

"It probably didn't feel right."

What can Tommy do to make him stop?

"Ask him to stop."

What does Tommy think about his uncle?

"He just loves him very much. His uncle cares how Tommy feels because Tommy is his nephew. If Tommy tells on his uncle, the uncle will punish him."

Pretend his uncle tells Tommy "Don't tell anybody what I did." Should Tommy keep the secret? Why?

"Yes, because he should obey his uncle."

Does Tammy's uncle care about her?

"Yes, because she could get sick if her uncle doesn't care."

Do you think Tammy and her uncle get along very well?

"Well, really, yes. Like he's taking care of her and likes to talk to her."

OLDER CHILDREN'S RISKS

It was expected that older children would "know better" than younger children. Overall, older children displayed less vulnerability than younger children. However, there was some support for the notion that vulnerability was not merely a function of chronological age. In general, Stage 1 reasoners displayed greater vulnerability than Stage 2 reasoners. Only in the case of resistance did advanced social reasoning make no difference. Level 2 reasoners were no more likely to display resistance than Level 1 reasoners, and the older Level 2 reasoners actually displayed a lower resistance rate than older Level 1 reasoners. Why would the "advanced" older children be less likely to offer resistance to a perpetrator?

The responses of five older Level 2 reasoners were examined. All five interviews revealed that these children responded to the Perpetrator Interview with "hedging" responses. For example, in response to the question, What is the problem in this story?, four of these subjects responded with some variation of "I *really* don't know." These children indicated that the main character should just go about the task at hand (i.e., go to bed, pick up the equipment, walk down the street) and *ignore* the perpetrator. Therefore, these older, advanced reasoners gave no overt indication of recognizing or resisting, yet they "knew." By their nonchalant responses, it seemed they were attempting to ignore and understate the obvious.

Rather than stating that the main character should ignore the perpetrator, the older children may have been endorsing such a response strategy by enacting it. Younger children and lower level reasoners seemed to enjoy overt identification of wrongdoing, as demonstrated by one young man who knowingly stated, "That stranger, he's a bad, tricky guy." For the older children, social maturity may demand that one "act cool" in the face of inappropriate activity.

The identification and field testing of effective resistance and reporting strategies, with a focus on the ages for which the strategies are best suited and the perpetrators against which they are most effective, would make a substantial contribution to prevention efforts. Table 5.1 specifies the most popular responses generated by the children of the Burkhardt study. Comparisons of child-generated responses with adult suggestions for resistance and reporting may identify differences between what children and adults consider effective.

IMPLICATIONS FOR PREVENTION

The children's own responses suggest numerous ways in which prevention programs can address recognition, resistance, and reporting. General findings include: (a) identifying and teaching rules about touching that emphasize children's notions about "wrongness"; (b) alerting children to the specific features of an interaction with a perpetrator, including trickery and unfair use of authority or power; and (c) increasing positive incentives for reporting by promising approval, praise, or rewards for reports. The use of child-generated strategies for teaching recognition, resistance, and reporting is recommended. Prevention efforts may be well served by helping children construct rationales for disobedience in response to related and unrelated perpetrators.

TREATMENT IMPLICATIONS OF A CHILD-GENERATED MODEL

Treatment of child victims and adult survivors of childhood sexual abuse demands clinicians to formulate hypotheses regarding what happened and why. Is

Table 5.1   Child-Generated Resistance and Reporting Strategies

Strategy	Child, Perpetrator
Say "What are you doing? Stop it."	(6-year-old boy, coach)
Say "Don't" and tell.	(7-year-old girl, coach)
Say "Don't do that."	(10-year-old boy, uncle)
Say "I don't really want to do this. Pick someone else."	(6-year-old girl, coach)
Say "No" and run.	(9-year-old boy, coach)
Tell him to stop it.	(6-year-old girl, uncle)
Tell him to cut it out.	(7-year-old girl, uncle)
Tell him not to do that.	(9-year-old girl, uncle)
Tell him to pick a different kid.	(9-year-old boy, coach)
Run away.	(6-year-old girl, coach)
Run away.	(9-year-old boy, stranger)
Run away and tell somebody.	(7-year-old boy, stranger)
Run away and get someone to help him.	(9-year-old boy, stranger)
Run, 'cuz his uncle is a fag.	(10-year-old boy, uncle)
She should say "no" because sometimes strangers act like that and want to take you.	(7-year-old girl, stranger)
Tammy should run away because she shouldn't even be talking to that man.	(6-year-old girl, stranger)
Tammy could maybe tell the man that she can't help—she might get lost and he could maybe find another girl.	(6-year-old girl, stranger)
Scream so people will hear and he'll stop.	(9-year-old girl, coach)
Scream. I wouldn't want my uncle to put his hand on my bottom.	(9-year-old girl, uncle)
Kick him in the face.	(8-year-old boy, coach)
Tell him to leave his hands off my private parts.	(7-year-old boy, coach)
Ask him to stop and move away.	(10-year-old girl, uncle)
Ask him to move.	(9-year-old boy, uncle)
Stop helping him.	(10-year-old boy, coach)
Go to mom and dad to buy another puppy.	(6-year-old boy, stranger)
Go home and see if his own puppy is gone.	(6-year-old boy, stranger)
Go home.	(9-year-old boy, coach)
Leave.	(7-year-old girl, coach)
Try getting away.	(7-year-old girl, stranger)
Tell somebody.	(11-year-old boy, coach)
Tell her mom and dad that a guy's trying to take her.	(10-year-old girl, stranger)
Tell her mom.	(9-year-old girl, uncle)
Tell him she feels sorry for him because he had a bad day.	(6-year-old girl, uncle)
Just run.	(9-year-old boy, coach)
Run away.	(10-year-old girl, coach)
Walk away from him.	(10-year-old boy, uncle)
Go to sleep.	(7-year-old boy, uncle)
Help find the puppy because the dog might get killed.	(6-year-old boy, stranger)

the client suffering from neurosis? Is he or she a product of a dysfunctional family? Is a lack of proper supervision rendering a child easy prey? An understanding of the vulnerability of average children to sexual abuse provides a norm against which clients' experiences and reasoning about those experiences can be compared. Several key features of children's reasoning about perpetrators have implications for professionals who treat child or adult victims of childhood sexual abuse:

1   Treatment may need to address the individual's reaction to feeling ineffective and unprotected.
A patient's treatment may be affected by the clinician's stance regarding an abusive encounter. Rapport may be disturbed and interpretations poorly received if the therapist misunderstands the client's thoughts and actions about the abuse. Beliefs that the client's ineffective responses to a perpetrator are due to pathology, as opposed to being a product of normal development, may be misguided, premature, or mistaken. Understanding the client's experiences is facilitated by therapist awareness of how typical children think and respond to childhood sexual abuse.

2   Childhood sexual abuse may contribute to the development of psychopathology.
Although the contributions of family dysfunction, psychopathology, and emotional disturbance to vulnerability to sexual abuse are not disputed, the Burkhardt study suggests another plausible explanation for a child being victimized. An average child could have the misfortune of encountering a perpetrator who overwhelms the child's social reasoning. Childhood sexual abuse is as likely to be a cause of psychopathology as a symptom of it. Although social reasoning may affect vulnerability to sexual abuse, conversely, normal development may be affected by abuse. Clinical reports indicate that adult survivors present with a variety of symptoms involving cognitive dysfunction, including dissociation, depersonalization, multiple personalities, and psychosis. Minimally, many victims of childhood sexual abuse are unable to form and maintain close interpersonal relationships and often have histories of repeated victimization.

Treatment should address the victim's disappointment at not being protected. If depression and anxiety are a result of forced helplessness, childhood sexual abuse is indeed a rich breeding ground for psychopathology. The Burkhardt study made children's expectations very clear: If children take action to resist and report, they expect their efforts to stop the perpetrator. Victims of actual sexual abuse, who have employed noble, but ineffective, childish forms of resistance and reporting, may be robbed of normal fantasies of omnipotence; they may be forced to confront the harsh reality that others can deceive, hurt, and confuse, and that no one can help.

LIMITATIONS OF A CHILD-GENERATED MODEL

The Burkhardt study served as the foundation for a child-generated model of sexual abuse intervention. The following limitations of the study and model are noted.

Reliance on Verbal Responses

The Burkhardt study relied on verbal responses to assess children's vulnerability to sexual abuse. Dependence on subjects' abilities to verbally articulate their reasoning is a limitation of most social cognitive research (Shantz, 1975). A researcher may underestimate a child's capabilities simply because the child does not possess sufficient linguistic skill to articulate the thoughts underlying his or her reasoning.

Unestablished Ability to Predict Actual Vulnerability

Just because a child states how to behave does not, of course, guarantee that he or she will behave that way. The research methodology employed in this study reveals only what children think. The design did not solicit actual performance of suggested responses. The use of a staged encounter with an authority figure issuing an abusive directive would have made it possible to determine the correlation between social cognition and performance—a key component in the formulation of effective prevention efforts. Although ethical constraints would preclude a sexually abusive directive, commands or requests regarding secret keeping or the use of deception by an adult could be followed by an interview aimed to determine the child's level of understanding about the adult and the encounter.

Limited Sample of Children

The Burkhardt study was conducted with a homogeneous population primarily consisting of White, middle-class youngsters. The generalizability of findings is, therefore, limited.

Properties of the Effectiveness Measures

Finally, in terms of methodological weakness, the reliability and validity of measures of effectiveness (i.e., highest effectiveness rating) have not been determined. These measures were included to assess qualitative differences in the way children respond to perpetrators. Further evaluation of the psychometric properties of the effectiveness measures is needed.

The validity of the effectiveness ratings of resistance and reporting strategies is of particular concern. Ratings were based on a consensus of scores assigned by female undergraduate students—at best only an estimate of what some adults believe about how children should respond to a perpetrator. Would these strategies actually stop a perpetrator? Although adults tell children to "just say no" or to report "if anybody tries to touch you," there is a distinct lack of empirical evidence regarding the feasibility or efficacy of such responses in an actual encounter (Melton, 1992a).

FUTURE RESEARCH

The Burkhardt study sought to investigate children's vulnerability to sexual abuse as a function of social reasoning. Unpredicted findings suggest avenues for future investigation.

Distinctions Among Types of Perpetrators

The children in the study made distinctions between the authority of a coach and that of a stranger. Still, comparisons of response rates for the Coach and Stranger groups failed to detect significant differences. A significant, but unpredicted difference was only revealed in the case of the younger children. The younger children were more likely to recognize a coach as a perpetrator than a stranger. It may be that the task of searching for a lost puppy was more appealing, and therefore more distracting, to children, compared with being a coach's helper and picking up equipment. It may be that going into the equipment room with a coach was a salient warning sign for the children that triggered recognition. The equivalent response rates of the Coach and Stranger groups suggest that children have at least two categories for adults: (a) those who are parents or like parents, and (b) those who are not.

Resistance Rates for Advanced Reasoners

A second set of unexpected findings was related to resistance rates. Overall, older children demonstrated higher response rates than younger children, but this finding was not true for resisting. Why did older children, who were more likely to recognize and report a perpetrator, fail to display greater resistance than the younger children? Similarly, children displaying Level 1 and Level 2 authority reasoning demonstrated equal rates of recognition and reporting, but older Level 1 reasoners were more likely to resist than older Level 2 reasoners. The question of why older children with lower level social reasoning outperformed age-mates with higher level reasoning remains unanswered.

Perhaps it is not "cool" to openly act as if one cannot handle a situation. What, if any, protective function this stance may serve for older children faced with a perpetrator requires further investigation. It may be that the older children with higher social reasoning were unwilling or unable to admit to facing a social situation that they could not handle. As older children face many unfamiliar adult social situations, perhaps feigning composure helps to mask underlying uncertainty. It may be that, as children mature, they act more knowledgeable than they really are as a means of self-protection. Further investigation of the relative regression demonstrated by the most mature subjects of the study is needed.

Boys' and Girls' Reasons for Responding

Review of individual interviews revealed that boys most frequently identified (a) fear of being labeled *homosexual* and (b) loss of privileges under the perpetrator's control as reasons for reluctance to report. Girls, particularly older girls, acted indignant about the perpetrator's actions. Differences in the ways boys and girls view sexual abuse and how to respond to a perpetrator need additional investigation.

Replication of Baseline Findings

The present study's methods and findings readily lend themselves to additional research efforts. Studies of this type with additional nonclinical populations would serve to replicate and expand on the baseline data generated by this sample. Longitudinal studies of children would afford an opportunity to track the progression of social cognitive development and vulnerability to abuse. In terms of design, studies in which children could be observed interacting with adult authority figures would improve the generalizability of findings.

Strategies of Real Victims of Childhood Sexual Abuse

Research with victims of childhood sexual abuse is needed to determine if these children display delayed or deviant social cognitive reasoning that might contribute to ongoing vulnerability to sexual abuse or disruption in interpersonal relationships. A comparison of the resistance and reporting strategies, offered by children who have actually responded to a perpetrator, with the responses of unmolested children to hypothetical dilemmas would make a significant step toward identifying effective strategies and highlighting potential risks and benefits.

UNDERSTANDING DEVELOPMENTAL VULNERABILITY

Vulnerability to perpetrators was found to be associated with age-appropriate social cognitive development in typical children. Vulnerability may be greater in some clinical populations, but average children are also at risk. The Burkhardt study demonstrated that some degree of vulnerability to childhood sexual abuse may be a basic part of being a child.

When an adult's directive is an appropriate one, an average child can produce a rationale for obedience. Such "rationalization" is not only adaptive, but a goal of socialization. However, if the directive is abusive, exploitive, self-serving, or deceptive, what is expected? Might a child still seek a rationale for obedience? Perhaps the automatic principles that govern social interactions with authority supersede the unique social demands of an abusive encounter—demands that require a rationale for disobedience of an adult directive.

The notion of developmental vulnerability is compatible with existing models of vulnerability. Finkelhor (1979) indicated that resources with children may serve to protect some from being targets of perpetrators, or that some children may mobilize their resources to rebuff a perpetrator's advances. Developmental vulnerability should be considered when evaluating why children fail to recognize, resist, and report.

Limited social reasoning constitutes a risk that may combine or interact with other identified risks factors to increase the possibility that abuse will occur in the first place and that perpetrators may proceed unchecked. Perpetrators may go unrecognized because children do not recognize abusive behavior. Perpetrators may proceed without resistance because children have no rationale for disobedience. Finally, perpetrators may remain unreported because children anticipate and weigh the consequences of telling.

The addition of developmental vulnerability does not exclude other risk factors. Psychopathology, such as mood or thought disorder, behavioral disorders, and emotional distress, may make unique contributions to vulnerability. Similarly, dysfunctional family environments may impact negatively on both social cognitive development and emotional stability, rendering children of such families distressed, needy, and unprepared to navigate social interactions with many adults, including a perpetrator. Biological factors, such as physical health, attractiveness, and puberty, may affect the way in which a perpetrator views a particular child. Finally, social and cultural forces that put children within the reach of perpetrators, that fail to remove known perpetrators from access to children, that value children who do not make trouble more than children who speak the truth, and that question the veracity of children who speak terrible truths will continue to put many children in harm's way.

By definition, children have emerging social cognitive reasoning abilities. What, then, if they are confronted with darkly complex social reasoning tasks, such as those involved in recognizing, resisting, and reporting an adult who approaches them in a sexual way? It is easy to say that, once warned, children should simply "know better" than to comply with an abusive directive or keep silent about what has happened. It is more realistic, however, to anticipate and plan for the limits of children's capabilities because perpetrators surely do.

SUMMARY

Existing formulations of vulnerability to childhood sexual abuse should be expanded to include developmental factors. The children of the Burkhardt study made distinctions about who should be obeyed and why. Understanding of legitimate and illegitimate uses of authority was evidenced by children of all ages. Many children considered the perpetrator's touching wrong, even if they did not know how a child should respond to it.

It seems likely that vulnerability to sexual abuse may vary with the authority of the perpetrator. In general, the greater the degree of authority or legitimacy attributed to an adult by a child, the greater the likelihood that a child will generate reasons for complying with the adult's directives, even abusive ones. The unfortunate combination of childhood vulnerability and the presence of perpetrators who seize opportunities and exploit vulnerability may lead to the development of sexually abusive interactions between a child and an abuser.

If resistance has been offered and has failed, or no resistance has been made by an overwhelmed child, abuse may occur. When a report is made by a child, or abuse is suspected or detected in any other way, the child may need to be assessed to determine what, if any, treatment is needed. How can caregivers respond to the abused child? A discussion of assessment (i.e., the gathering of information about the abused child) is found in chapter 6.

Assessment of Child Sexual Abuse

After prevention efforts have failed, but before treatment begins, a sexually abused child may require an assessment. The assessment of child sexual abuse must be detailed and comprehensive in nature because of the variables that are frequently correlated with it. Because of the complex nature of child abuse, a number of evaluation areas have to be addressed (e.g., cognitive, developmental, emotional, behavioral). Typically, the evaluation is made by a multidisciplinary team; however, one clinician should be responsible for assimilating and filing the data. Because there is a considerable amount of contact with the family, a social worker is generally assigned this role.

Standardized and informal evaluation procedures are used to gather information. At all times, the clinicians involved in the evaluation process should remain objective toward the child, the abuser, the family, and the abuse experience. This is critical to protect the child and the family. Additionally, clinicians must be cognizant that the evaluation of child sexual abuse is full of entangling problems, including that an estimated 2%–8% of all allegations of child sexual abuse are false (Kaplan & Sadock, 1991). Other problems include the following: a high number of cases cannot be proved, evaluation errors are made by inexperienced clinicians, allegations of child sexual abuse are made as a strategy in custody hearings to limit a caregiver's visitation rights, preschool children's verbal skills often limit a valid description of the abuse, and leading questions are often interjected during the evaluation process (Kaplan & Sadock, 1991). In

Table 6.1   Definitions of Child Sexual Abuse

Author(s)	Definition
Baker and Duncan (1985)	A child (anyone under 16 years) is sexually abused when another person, who is sexually mature, involves the child in any activity that the other person expects to lead to their sexual arousal. (p. 458)
Mrazek and Mrazek (1981)	The sexual use of a child by an adult for his or her sexual gratification without consideration of the child's psychological sexual development. (p. 80)
Schechter and Roberge (1976)	The involvement of dependent, developmentally immature children and adolescents in sexual activities they do not truly comprehend, to which they are unable to give informed consent or that violate the social taboos of the family roles. (p. 60)

this chapter, a working rationale and framework for collecting data for the initial evaluation of child sexual abuse is provided. The contents include information on terminology, statistics on occurrence, warning signs frequently associated with child sexual abuse, interview and testing procedures, and factors to consider when making assessment decisions. For purposes of clarification, the broad definition of *child sexual abuse* adopted by the National Center on Child Abuse and Neglect (NCCAN) in 1978 is used (see chap. 1, this volume).

Although other definitions exist (see Table 6.1), Glaser and Frosh (1988) stated that three major points tend to be central to these definitions: the act is carried out for the adult's sexual gratification, an element of "unwantedness of the sexual contact by the child" exists, and sexual abuse involves exploitation of a power differential.

TERMINOLOGY

Categories

An accurate evaluation and diagnosis of child sexual abuse requires a clinician to be aware of different categories of child sexual abuse. These categories include: incest, molestation, rape, statutory rape, pedophilia, child prostitution, child pornography, and exhibitionism. These areas are each described in turn.

Incest is defined as any physical sexual activity between closely related persons. These persons may be members of the child's immediate family, but blood relationship is not required. Thus, incest could involve stepfathers, stepmothers, and nonrelated siblings living in a home. Furthermore, incest would include close family members who live outside of the home, such as grandparents, uncles, or married older siblings. Although incest may be present among closely related adults, the present emphasis is on children from preschool age to adolescence.

Kaplan and Sadock (1991) reported that 75% of incest cases involve daughter and natural father. Although sibling incest is relatively low, mental health professionals have stressed that it is often denied by parents or may involve normal sexual play and exploration (see Glasser & Frosh, 1988; Russell, 1983; Siegel, Sorenson, Golding, Burnam, & Stein, 1987; Wyatt, 1985).

Molestation is defined as a disturbing or annoying unwarranted sexual act toward a child. This would include acts such as excessive touching or hugging, fondling the child's breast or genital areas, masturbatory stimulation, or encouraging a child to fondle or masturbate the adult. Kempe and Kempe (1984) stressed that these activities increase in frequency with time, and can lead to mutual masturbation or oral–genital contact.

Rape is an act of violence and humiliation that involves forcible sexual intercourse without the partner's consent. The legal definition of rape in the United States is:

> The perpetration of an act of sexual intercourse with a female, not one's wife, against her will and consent, whether her will is overcome by force or fear, resulting from the threat of force or by drugs or intoxicants; or when because of mental deficiency she is incapable of exercising rational judgement, or when she is below an arbitrary age of consent. (Kaplan & Sadock, 1991, p. 461)

When a person is below the age of consent, regardless of whether force was used, the act is defined as *statutory rape*. Kaplan and Sadock stressed that the legal definition of rape ''requires slight penile penetration of the victim's outer vulva and full erection and ejaculation are not necessary'' (p. 461). Last, Sarason and Sarason (1984) pointed out that victims can be either male or female, yet national statistics indicate females are more likely to be victims.

Sexual intercourse, according to Kempe and Kempe (1984), can involve ''statutory rape with a child of either sex, including fellatio (oral–genital contact), or penile–vaginal intercourse, may occur without physical violence through seduction, persuasion, bribes, use of authority or other threats'' (p. 11). These authors stated that, although the legal consent age for intercourse varies from state to state (e.g., 12–18), the psychological impact on the child is the primary concern.

Pedophilia involves an adult's intense sexual cravings or arousal for prepubertal children. The term *pedophile* may be used to describe an individual who actually molests children, but it also appropriately applies to individuals who fantasize about sexual activity with children (American Psychiatric Association, 1994). Kaplan and Sadock (1991) noted that the diagnosis may be clinically warranted for a perpetrator younger than 16 years of age when information demonstrates this category of sexual abuse. Kempe and Kempe (1984) emphasized that the sexual activity is broad and includes any form of sexual abuse in which the child is a "participant–object" of the activity.

Child prostitution involves the practice of children receiving money for engaging in sex acts. Child prostitutes can be either female or male. Young male prostitutes are called *chickens*. Dacey and Kenny (1994) reported that parental neglect and abuse are quite typical of teenage girls who become prostitutes. Additionally, Gibson-Ainyette, Templer, and Brown (1988) pointed out that many child prostitutes have been victims of rape, incest, and child molestation, which leads to a negative attitude toward themselves, the opposite sex, and their bodies.

Child pornography, according to Kempe and Kempe (1984), involves:

> the arranging, photographing by still, video, or film production of any material involving minors in sexual acts including other children, adults, or animals, regardless of consent by the child's legal guardian, and the distribution of such material in any form, with or without profit, and the exhibition of such material, with or without profit. (pp. 12–13)

These authors emphasized that many states have laws against child pornography, and that in 1982 the Supreme Court upheld the rights of states to outlaw such activity.

Exhibitionism is the exposure of one's genitals to a stranger or an unsuspecting individual. The *DSM–IV* diagnostic criteria for exhibitionism include exposure fantasies or behaviors (American Psychiatric Association, 1994). According to Kaplan and Sadock (1991), the person exposes himself "to assert his masculinity by showing his penis and by watching the reaction of the victim— fright, surprise, disgust" (p. 445). Exhibitionism can start prior to adolescence, but the peak age period for this sexual act is during the twenties (Sarason & Sarason, 1984). In practically all cases, it is males exposing themselves to females.

OCCURRENCE OF CHILD SEXUAL ABUSE

A comprehensive 50-state survey on victimization of children indicated that 404,100 children between the ages of birth to 17 were sexually abused during 1990 (see Daro & McCurdy, 1991). This rate was 6.3% of the population. The sexual abuse occurred in all geographic areas, among all races, and at all socioeconomic levels. Furthermore, a number of studies have consistently reported that child sexual abuse tends to be concentrated among teenagers (see Cantwell, 1981; Powers & Eckenrode, 1992; Sedlak, 1991). However, Finkelhor and Dziuba-Leatherman (1994) stressed that the statistics reported are an artifact of national studies because the rate was based on reported cases. In fact, when an examination of rates incorporates data from an examination of self-reports, about

64% of child sexual abuse occurs before age 12 (Finkelhor, Hotaling, Lewis, & Smith, 1990). This statistic fits better, according to Finkelhor and Dziuba-Leatherman, because acts of child victimization tend to occur more frequently due to the child's dependency situation. In other words, the more dependent one is, the greater the likelihood of being victimized.

Plummer (1984) wrote that about one in five children in the typical classroom has encountered sexual abuse, and that in 70%–80% of the cases the offenders are known to the children. Also, more girls are sexually abused than boys. Nationally, girls are twice as likely to be sexually abused as boys (Finkelhor & Dziuba-Leatherman, 1994). Interestingly, this rate does not change during adolescence, when one might expect girls to be more vulnerable as they age (see Finkelhor & Dziuba-Leatherman, 1994). As discussed in chapter 1, the differential rate of sexual abuse between girls and boys has to be examined in light of reports that the sexual abuse of male children is underreported (see Peake, 1989; Rew & Esparza, 1990). Wurtele and Miller-Perrin (1992) listed the following reasons for underreporting: "(a) societal expectations for boys to be dominant and self-reliant; (b) societal notions that early sexual experiences are a normal part of boys' lives; (c) boys' fears of being considered homosexual, since most boys are abused by men; and (d) societal pressures on males not to express helplessness or vulnerability" (p. 10). Wurtele and Miller-Perrin (1992) went on to report that the more current literature is reporting a higher proportion of males being abused (see Abel et al., 1987; Gale, Thompson, Moran, & Sack, 1988; Sedlak, 1991).

Wurtele and Miller-Perrin (1992) indicated that the prevalence of childhood sexual abuse among clinical populations is higher than among nonclinical populations. Table 6.2 shows the rates among various clinical populations. Although large-scale prevalence studies have not been carried out, the rates reveal a serious problem because of the recent literature, which documents that childhood sexual abuse has immediate and long-term effects on a child's socioemotional health (Finkelhor & Dziuba-Leatherman, 1994). For example, Saunders, Villeponteaux, Lipovsky, Kilpatrick, and Veronen (1992) reported that childhood sexual abuse presents a fourfold increased lifetime risk for any psychiatric disorder and a threefold risk for substance abuse. Furthermore, Scott (1992) estimated that close to 8% of all mental illness cases can be attributed to childhood sexual abuse.

In addition to the mental health damage that appears to stem from child sexual abuse, there is growing concern regarding the physical injuries that result from acts of child sexual abuse. For example, the National Study of the Incidence and Severity of Child Abuse and Neglect, 1988 (Sedlak, 1991) reported that about 5% of sexually abused children sustain physical injuries. Also, older children may contract a human immunodeficiency virus (HIV) infection from the sexual abuse because they suffer more penetrative abuse (see Kerns & Ritter, 1991).

Table 6.2   Prevalence Rates of Childhood Sexual Abuse Reported by Clinical Populations

Authors	Clinical population	Rates (%)
Briere and Zaidi (1989)	Outpatient psychiatric (Emergency Room)	70
Bliss (1984)	Multiple personality disorder	
Bryer, Nelson, Miller, and Krol (1987)	Borderline personality disorder	52
Coons, Bowman, Pellow, and Schneider (1989)	Posttraumatic stress disorder	57
Coons and Milstein (1986)	Multiple personality disorder	73
Dell and Eisenhower (1990)	Multiple personality disorder	75
Drossman et al. (1990)	Gastrointestinal disorder	30
Hall, Tice, Beresford, Wooley, and Hall (1989)	Anorexia or bulimia	50
Herman, Perry, and van der Kolk (1989)	Borderline personality disorder	55
Jacobson and Herald (1990)	Psychiatric inpatients	26 (males) 54 (females)
Paddison et al. (1990)	Premenstrual syndrome	22
Rohsenow, Corbett, and Devine (1988)	Female inpatient substance abusers	77
Western, Ludolph, Misle, Ruffins, and Block (1990)	Borderline personality disorder	60
Wurtele, Kaplan, and Keairnes (1990)	Female chronic pain patients	39

SYMPTOMS AND SIGNS OF CHILD SEXUAL ABUSE

Clinicians who suspect child sexual abuse must be aware of the physical and behavioral warning signs. Rotatori and Day (1990) listed the following indicators: difficulty walking or sitting; complaints of pain or itching in the genital area; bleeding or bruises in genital area; presence of sexually transmitted disease; pregnancy; torn, stained, or bloody underclothing; frequent urinary infections; more sexually aware than peers; fear of malls; and seductive toward males. A more comprehensive listing by Glaser and Frosh (1988) appears in Table 6.3. Their listing provides symptoms and signs of sexual abuse in three major areas: physical manifestations, emotional and behavioral manifestations, and family relationship patterns. Additionally, Glaser and Frosh identified six symptoms and eight signs that are highly suggestive of child sexual abuse. According to these authors, symptoms are "outcomes about which the child is aware and which may indeed cause discomfort and lead to seeking medical or other help. . . . Signs are those manifestations which are observed by others" (Glaser & Frosh, 1988, p. 62).

Table 6.3   Signs and Symptoms of Child Sexual Abuse

Aspect of abuse	Manifestations
	Physical
Trauma	Vulvovaginal soreness or discomfort (sy, si)
	Vaginal bleeding in pre-pubertal girls (sy)*
	Genital laceration (si)*
	Bruising in genital area (si)*
	Enlarged vaginal opening, scarred hymen (si)*
	Vaginal discharge (sy, si)
	Lax or pouting anal sphincter, anal fissures or scars (si)*
	Rectal bleeding (sy)
	Fecal soiling or retention (sy)
	Discomfort on micturition and recurrent urinary tract infections (sy, si)
	Evidence of child abuse (si)
Infection	Sexually transmitted disease, including genital warts (sy, si)*
	Vaginal discharge (sy)
Sexual intercourse	Pregnancy (particularly when identity of father is uncertain) (sy, si)*
	Emotional and behavioral
Premature sexualism	Explicit or frequent sexual preoccupation in talk and play (si)**
	Sexualization of relationships (si)*
	Premature sexual awareness (si)**
	Undue avoidance of men (si)*
	Masturbation (si)
Experiences of guilt, confusion, anxiety, fear, anger	Hints of possession of secrets (sy)*
	Running away from home (sy)*
	Parasuicide (sy)*
	Child psychiatric problems (sy, si)
	Learning difficulties (si)
	Family relationship patterns
	Distant mother–child relationship
	Parentified child
	Parental conflict
	Unclear intergenerational boundaries
	Child abuse
	Alcohol abuse

Note. From *Child Sexual Abuse* (p. 62) by D. Glaser and S. Frosh, 1988, Chicago: Dorsey Press. Copyright 1988 by Dorsey Press. Reprinted by permission.

sy = symptom; si = sign.

*highly suggestive of child sexual abuse (lack of * denotes a nonspecific, but possible alerting sign).

**a learned pattern.

Table 6.4   Behavioral, Emotional, and Physical Indicators of Sexual Abuse According to Level of Development

Sexual abuse indicators	Preschool (0–5 yrs)	School age (6–12 yrs)	Adolescence (13–16 yrs)
Behavioral			
Regression	X		
Social withdrawal	X	X	X
Preoccupation with sex	X	X	X
Knowledge of sexual acts	X	X	X
Seductive behavior	X	X	X
Excessive masturbation	X	X	
Sex play with others	X	X	
Sexual language	X	X	X
Genital exposure	X	X	
Victimizing others	X	X	X
Promiscuity/prostitution			X
Difficulty separating	X		
Delinquency		X	X
Stealing		X	X
Running away		X	X
Early marriage			X
Substance abuse		X	X
Truancy			X
Dropping out of school			X
Learning difficulties		X	X
Poor concentration/ attention		X	X
Declining grades		X	X
Poor peer relations		X	X
Emotional			
Anxiety	X	X	X
Clinging	X		
Nightmares	X	X	X
Fear of adults	X	X	
Phobias		X	X
Obsessions		X	X
Tics		X	

(Continued)

Wurtele and Miller-Perrin (1992) stressed that "symptoms of child sexual abuse do not follow a set pattern, nor do all child victims display the same kinds of behaviors" (p. 103). However, it is critical for parents and clinicians to be aware of potential signs of child sexual abuse. As a means to develop a list of indicators, Wurtele and Miller-Perrin reviewed over 40 articles on this topic. Their list (see Table 6.4) delineates symptoms by category as well as developmental level. Wurtele and Miller-Perrin offered the following guidelines when using the list: (a) an indicator becomes more significant when it represents a

Table 6.4 Behavioral, Emotional, and Physical Indicators of Sexual Abuse According to Level of Development *(Continued)*

Sexual abuse indicators	Developmental level		
	Preschool (0–5 yrs)	School age (6–12 yrs)	Adolescence (13–16 yrs)
Depression	X	X	X
Guilt	X	X	X
Suicidal ideation			X
Suicide attempts		X	X
Low self-esteem/ confidence			X
Hostility/anger	X	X	X
Tantrums	X		
Aggression	X	X	
Family/peer conflicts	X	X	
Physical			
Bruises/genital bleeding	X		
Genital pain/itching/odors	X	X	X
Problems walking/sitting	X	X	X
Sleep disturbance	X	X	X
Appetite disturbance	X	X	X
Somatic concerns	X	X	X
Enuresis	X	X	
Encopresis	X	X	
Stomachaches	X	X	X
Headaches	X	X	X
Pregnancy			X

Note. From *Preventing Child Sexual Abuse: Sharing the Responsibility* (pp. 105-106) by S. K. Wurtele and C. L. Miller-Perrin, 1992, Lincoln, NE: University of Nebraska Press. Copyright 1992 by University of Nebraska Press. Reprinted by permission.

radical change in the child's typical behavior, (b) symptoms that are chronic and resistive to typical intervention are more indicative of underlying child sexual abuse, (c) patterns of symptoms have more relevance than solo symptoms, and (d) the severity of the symptoms are more indicative of child sexual abuse.

VARIABLES RELATED TO CHILD SEXUAL ABUSE

Clinicians need to be cognizant of environmental and familial variables that tend to be indicators of child sexual abuse. Table 6.5 was devised after examining a number of works that have discussed such variables in detail (see Glaser & Frosh, 1988; Kempe & Kempe, 1984; Wurtele & Miller-Perrin, 1992). The indicators are grouped under three headings: parent, home environment, and child–parent. The clinician is cautioned that the presence of these indicators is not a direct causal relationship because there "are no pathognomonic indicators of sexual abuse victimization" (Wurtele & Miller-Perrin, 1992, p. 152). How-

Table 6.5   Variables Related to Child Sexual Abuse

Parent	Home environment	Child–parent
Marital discord	Stress from employment	Child's hold on parent in family
Power imbalance	Social isolation	Emotional neglect
Poor impulse control	Mother is absent for some overriding reason (e.g., chronic illness)	Weak early father–daughter attachment
Alcohol abuse history	Over- or undersexualization	Inappropriate expectations of child's responsibilities
Parental history of sexual abuse	Household crowding	Distant mother–daughter relationship
Poor parental modeling of self-protective behaviors	Chaotic sleeping arrangements	Weak or absent parent–child bonding
Sexually promiscuous lifestyle of parents	Stress from poverty	Inefficient or sporadic supervision
Parents do not have close friendships	Lack of privacy	Exploitation serving adult needs
Absence of a natural parent		
Presence of a father substitute		

ever, the presence of these indicators with those listed in Table 6.4 should allow clinicians more success in child sexual abuse identification cases.

DATA COLLECTION, TESTING, AND INTERVIEW PROCEDURES

Rotatori, Steckler, Fox, and Green (1984) developed a data recording form that can be used by a multidisciplinary team to examine allegations of child abuse. The form provides for data collection in five major domains: social, medical, educational, intellectual, and personality. Information collected in the social domain is directed at three areas: (a) child problems (e.g., cries frequently, frequently noncompliant), (b) parent problems (e.g., immoral behavior, alcohol abuse, separation), and (c) adult parenting (e.g., lack knowledge, refuse family needs). The medical domain provides for information in five areas: physical injury, malnutrition, gynecological exam, neurological exam, and ophthalmological exam. Information in the educational domain is collected in school be-

Table 6.6   Sample of Items from the Carroll and Van Dornick (1984) Data Collection Sexual Abuse Record

Item
Was there marital collusion in alleged sexual abuse? Degree to which father acknowledged harm done to child by sexual abuse: 　—Denied or failed to recognize actual or potential abuse. 　—Acknowledged actual or potential harm. Was father sexually abused as a child? Yes _____ No _____ 　—Specifics of age, perpetrator, duration, and treatment: _____ Mother's response to disclosure of incest: _____ Is the child provocative sexually or seductive? 　　Mother's impression _____ 　　Father's impression _____ 　　Evaluator's impression _____ Other sexual activity of child (i.e., masturbation, sexual play, sexually active with peers):
Rate stress affecting family household: job difficulties, loss of job, disrupting physical illness of household members, death of close family member, residence in substandard housing.

havior (e.g., sexual acting out, frequency of noncompliance) and academic achievement. The intellectual domain is directed at gathering descriptive information about a child's cognitive ability and developmental status. In the personality domain, information is gathered to describe the child's affect and emotional status.

SOCIAL DOMAIN

Typically, a social worker is assigned the task of collecting social domain information. The first step is compiling a comprehensive social history. Information is gathered from interviews of family members and informants. It is necessary to contact the local child protective service agency to document whether a prior record of child sexual abuse, neglect, or physical abuse has occurred.

A highly recommended form for interviewing family members is the Data Collection Sexual Abuse Record, developed by Carroll and Van Dornick (1984). This record has 146 items, including information on the following: child identifying information, child characteristics, type and length of sexual abuse, the child's perception of sexual abuse, parents' characteristics, parents' explanation of sexual abuse, parents' level of emotional functioning and mental health status, family characteristics, and attributes of the family household. A sample of items from the record appear in Table 6.6.

The Sexual Abuse Screening Inventory (SASI; McCoy, 1987) is another form that can be used to collect social information. The SASI is divided into eight categories or groupings: school, peer, adult relations, bedtime habits, hy-

Table 6.7   Highly Significant Indicators of Abuse from the Sexual Abuse Screening Inventory (McCoy, 1987)

Indicator
1. Initiates sexual games with peers.
2. Touches peers excessively or on private parts.
3. Touches adults excessively or inappropriately.
4. Makes inappropriate sexual remarks or comments.
5. Keeps a weapon such as a knife or club close by bed.
6. Tries to spy on or intrudes on others in the bathroom.
7. Runs away or threatens to run away.
8. Shows regressive behavior (i.e., enuresis).
9. Is sexually active.
10. Has knowledge of sexual activity inappropriate to age level.
11. Excessively masturbates for age level.
12. Displays extreme fear of a certain place or person.

giene, behavioral/emotional, medical, and miscellaneous. Sixty-one items can be examined to ascertain the presence of certain behaviors or indicators. Items that are highly indicative of sexual abuse appear in Table 6.7.

Information from the social domain provides an accurate social assessment of the strengths and weaknesses that the child, parents, and family members possess. Such information provides insights into situational variables that have led to acts of sexual abuse, as well as determines intervention practices and prognosis. For example, dealing with a sexual abuse incident is more encouraging in situations where a child has developed basic trust, autonomy, and a good self-concept than with a child who is untrusting, dependent, and lacking in self-confidence and self-esteem. Also, in home environments where the child's feelings have been nurtured and recognized, the opportunity for a more positive outcome is present than in a family environment in which marital strife or the parents' preoccupation with their own emotionality is paramount.

Data from this domain can be used to pinpoint: (a) problematic social-interactional patterns with the family and the immediate neighborhood; (b) characteristics of the child, parents, and family members that are correlated with child sexual abuse; and (c) situational stress factors that are often linked to sexual abuse. For example, the information may indicate that the sexual abuse is more frequent when mother works on weekends or when father has periods of unemployment. In other cases, the information may reveal that the family maintains "very loose intergenerational boundaries and appear underorganized, one aspect of which may be chaotic sleeping arrangements . . . child sexual abuse may be one correlate of cross-generational confusions" (Glaser & Frosh, 1988, p. 65). Also, in some situations, there is a confusion of boundaries, where the parent and child may be acting on a peer level (see Plummer, 1984). At other times, boundaries are confused, such that the parent and child cannot determine where the boundaries begin and end (e.g., such as the father who believes that the child's body is his property). Last, information may reveal that positive support of significant others is present, which has been found to help victims adjust in extrafamilial child sexual assault and incest cases.

MEDICAL EXAM CONCERNS

The medical examination of a child who has been reported to be sexually abused is a necessity. However, clinicians should realize that there is conflicting opinion about this. Some professionals state that the exam can be quite upsetting to the child because it is often perceived as an unwarranted assault. However, law enforcement personnel believe the exam is critical in the substantiation of the sexual abuse. Although the exam is recommended, clinicians need to be aware that less than half of the children examined for sexual abuse have any positive findings at the time of the exam (Glaser & Frosh, 1988).

Fontana (1982) specified that the attending physician has the responsibility to explain to the child and parents what to expect from the medical exam. Part of the exam involves the interrogation of the child to ascertain specific information, such as the date, time, place, and alleged perpetrator, and a description of the act (e.g., ejaculation in the mouth). In most cases, a social worker or sexual abuse counselor is assigned to gather descriptive information. When collecting this information, Bass and Davis (1988) listed the following questions to consider for the interrogation:

> Touched in sexual areas?
> Shown sexual movies or forced to listen to sexual talk?
> Subjected to unnecessary medical treatments?
> Forced to perform oral sex on an adult or sibling?
> Raped or otherwise penetrated?
> Fondled, kissed, or held in a way that made you uncomfortable?
> Forced to take part in ritualized abuse in which you were physically or sexually tortured?
> Made to watch sexual acts or look at sexual parts?
> Bathed in a way that felt intrusive to you?
> Objectified and goaded into sex you didn't really want?
> Told all you were good for was sex?
> Involved in child prostitution or pornography? (p. 22)

Other critical questions involve who may have witnessed the abuse, child's feelings about being sexually abused, child's feelings toward the abuser, and whether the child has been told to keep the acts a secret or been threatened with harm for divulging any information (Glaser & Frosh, 1988).

This information is gathered in the presence of a trusted person (e.g., person who has disclosed information to authorities). Generally this is the child's mother. However, it may be an aunt or grandparent. Most clinicians agree that the facilitation of the interview process is much greater when this trusted person is present (Glaser & Collins, 1987).

When interrogating young children below the age of 7, anatomically correct rag dolls, drawings, and play materials can be used as an aid for the child to communicate any alleged sexual abuse. These aids should not be considered diagnostic tools (see Glaser & Frosh, 1988), but rather vehicles for the victimized child to provide the examiner with the facts and circumstances of the abuse in a nonthreatening and nonjudgmental atmosphere. The child may be asked to draw a picture of the sexual abuse incident and identify the persons by printing the names if possible. This is often less traumatic for the child than stating the facts and names verbally.

Shamroy (1982) indicated that, when using dolls, it is critical that a common mode of communication regarding body parts be established. This can be done by pointing to a body part and asking the child what it is called. Once this mode has been established, the examiner can request that the child demonstrate what happened.

Although this information is useful, Solnit, Nordhaus, and Lard (1992) stressed that:

> there are at present no reliable data to suggest that play with such dolls can be interpreted as an accurate historical rendering of an experience a child has had. All children—whether abused or not—have fantasies about their own and their parents' sexuality. These can be misunderstood or assessed incorrectly by individuals not trained to understand children and their play. (p. 84)

Although caution is recommended, information from doll play is valuable in terms of a clinical expectation of what nonabused and abused children demonstrate in such sessions. For example, Glaser and Frosh (1988) reported that sexually abused children were more likely than nonabused children to demonstrate the following: (a) roughly treating adult male doll, (b) quickly and without hesitancy undressing dolls, (c) placing the dolls in sexually oriented positions after undressing them, (d) inserting finger into vaginal or anal opening, and (e) enacting explicit sexual activity between the dolls. In contrast, Glaser and Collins (1987) reported that nonabused children are extremely hesitant to undress the dolls, even when given instructions to do so, and they rarely enact adult sexual activity when playing with the dolls.

The interview information needs to be written down accurately because it may serve as evidence in a possible court case (Kempe & Kempe, 1984). Also, Fontana (1982) recommended that the child be informed of the medical exam and what will take place. The child's need for privacy should be respected at all times, and the child should be guaranteed that there will be no reprisals.

Glaser and Frosh (1988) stressed that the medical exam should be done in a calm and unhurried manner. They indicated that sedation of the child is generally not needed. Glaser and Frosh stressed that, during the examination,

the child's response to the examination, particularly of the genitalia, may provide
an indication of the emotional effect of the abuse. Some children will strenuously
resist examination, indicating the degree of traumatization. Others will accede too
readily, assuming sexualized postures and indicating the degree of habituation which
regular abuse has caused them. (p. 104)

Fontana (1982) recommended that:

The pelvic examination, in the case of a girl, should be gentle and should include a
careful inspection of the external genitalia, the urethra, vagina, cervix, and anus.
The presence of sperm can be determined by inserting a moistened cotton-tipped
applicator into the vagina; the applicator is then spread on a slide. The physician
records any evidences of trauma to the anus and external genitalia in the form of
abrasions, purpura and petechiae (large and small "blood blisters"), tears, and areas
of inflammation. The hymenal ring should be inspected documenting the diameter
of the opening, and the presence of fresh tears or old scars. Laboratory tests for the
presence of semen are necessary to substantiate incest or rape. Additional laboratory
procedures, including endocervical, pharyngeal, and rectal cultures should be undertaken to ascertain the possible existence of such venereal diseases as gonorrhea,
syphilis, or genital herpes. The finding of a vaginal discharge or an inflamed perineal
area should lead to a culture for gonorrhea. Any evidence of anal trauma or manip-
ulation calls for a sperm test and gonorrheal cultures of this site. Sexual abuse should
be suspected in any young child having a history of vaginitis, inflammation of the
vagina, or vaginal discharge. (p. 12)

EDUCATIONAL DOMAIN

The child's school records should be examined to identify changes in levels of
performance and behavior. For example, a sudden decrease in academic performance and attentiveness may be due to the child's preoccupation "with fantasies
or anxiety related to the sexual abuse and its consequences" (Kempe & Kempe,
1984, p. 118). In contrast, long-standing child sexual abuse has been linked to
"learning difficulty, declining grades and difficulties with concentration and
attention, and poor peer relations" (Wurtele & Miller-Perrin, 1992, pp. 104–
105). In addition, acting out behaviors, such as delinquency, stealing, running
away, and substance abuse, have been noted.

It is recommended that the child be observed in the classroom to collect
information on the presence of problems in attention to task, concentration,
persistence, response to feedback, tolerance level, fluency in communicating
during class discussions, and degree to which child is motivated by praise and
rewards (Rotatori & Day, 1990). After this information is generated, standardized achievement testing should be carried out to validate present levels of
academic functioning in reading, arithmetic, and general knowledge. Because
the child may be anxious, due to the reported sexual abuse situation, the interpretation of his or her performance must be governed by caution.

COGNITIVE DOMAIN

A sexually abused child's cognitive capacity should be measured by administering a standardized intelligence test. This evaluation procedure is recommended when a child's grades have declined significantly, or when educational achievement on recent standardized academic tests fall below the child's grade level. Administration of an intelligence test should provide information to explain a discrepancy between the child's intellectual capacity and academic achievement. Also, this information is

> useful to know whether lower than expected achievement in school, if any, was always present (indicating preceding problems), whether it occurred after the onset of sexual abuse, or whether the child's school performance was unaffected by the sexual abuse. Good individual psychological testing gives evidence of how a child copes, of the ability to deal with mild stress, to organize and use information, and to overcome impatience or discouragement during the course of a test. (Kempe & Kempe, 1984, p. 132)

Rotatori and Day (1990) cautioned that the literature on abused children reveals the following characteristics that may impact test score interpretation: higher verbal skills than motor skills (see Berger, 1981), greater distractibility during the testing (see Friedrich, Einbender, & Luecke, 1983), and higher rates of negative, unresponsive, stubborn, and impulsive behavior (see Johnson & Morse, 1968).

COLLECTING PERSONALITY DATA

It is vital to assess a child's present affective dimension to determine whether the sexual victimization has resulted in any temporary or long-lasting psychological damage. Personality assessment provides data useful in recommendations regarding the form and intensity of therapeutic emotional intervention, if needed. Kempe and Kempe (1984) indicated five major affective aspects that should be examined: (a) fears, (b) anxiety level, (c) feelings of vulnerability, (d) separation and loss of nurturance, and (e) shame and guilt. In addition, it is necessary to identify what reaction mechanism the child displays to inner affective environment. For example, Kempe and Kempe related that, although all sexually abused children experience some anger, the direction their anger takes can vary depending on the particular abuse. If the abuse is clear-cut and the family and authorities blame the offender, children will be more open about expressing their anger at the offender. However, when the sexual abuse has been ongoing, with the child not reporting it, the child may experience considerable anger but also fear about reporting it to anyone. According to Kempe and Kempe, this latter situation may result in the anger being displaced (i.e., with the child expressing it via depression or social acting out). For some sexually abused children, the acting out may take the form of "repetitive sexually aggressive behavior or preoccupation with sexual anatomy and feelings . . . masturbatory behavior that is excessive and unusual when compared to peers, sometimes including penetration with objects or repeated attempts to engage others in sexual behaviors" (Corwin, 1988, p. 257).

Generally, sexually abused children tend to deny or avoid their emotional reactions related to being sexually victimized (see Corwin, 1988). Because of this latter aspect, human figure drawings have been relied on to ascertain a sexually abused child's inner affective dimensions. Miller and Veltkamp (1989) reported that the research literature strongly suggests that sexually abused children tend to draw figures that focus on sexually relevant body parts. Furthermore, these drawings can assist the court in understanding the processing of training by the child and rendering a decision that is in the child's best interests. However, Hagood (1988) pointed out that, although they have been helpful to clinicians, there are many problems associated with projective drawings. For example, drawing tests are used as a preliminary assessment tool and are often interpreted on an analytical basis. Also, frequently only one drawing is used, and drawings are often discussed with other professionals on their own merit without corroboration by the child. Hagood stressed that serious reliability and validity problems are major drawbacks in using children's figure drawings as an accurate assessment instrument.

Hagood (1988) provided some excellent insights for interpreting a child's drawings. For example, a phenomenon that frequently occurs in the drawings and sculptures of young sexually abused children is the depiction of anatomically correct male genitalia, which sometimes includes ejaculation and is created at a level of realism far beyond developmental appropriateness. Also, sexually abused children usually name the genitalia as some other object, such as a tree, a cloud, or a heart, just to name a few. According to Hagood, the naming of the phalluses as some other object has two explanations: (a) the child is conscious of what he or she has drawn, but attempts to disguise this knowledge; or (b) the phallus as the traumatic object is unconsciously portrayed. This author has mentioned that a considerable amount of further investigation needs to be done to understand this phenomenon and to learn whether it occurs in drawings of non-abused children as well.

Howe, Burgess, and McCormack (1987) reported a comprehensive study on the image characteristics and artistic properties of the drawings of adolescent runaways who had been sexually victimized. The study sample consisted of 149 runaway adolescents living in a Canadian crisis shelter. Of the sample, 51% reported having been sexually abused, with the incidence of abuse for females being higher than that for males. Each subject, after being interviewed and administered several standardized tests, was asked to draw a whole person on a piece of white paper. The subjects were allowed to choose pencil, pen, or crayons as drawing instruments. The drawings were then independently evaluated by three art therapists. The therapists used five assessment indicators: gender, figure completion, integrity of line quality, use of color, and graphic indicators of sexual anxiety. For gender, the figures were coded by gender of the subject and by gender of the figure drawn. It was found that females who were sexually abused were more likely to draw a figure of the opposite sex than were males.

For the indicator of figure completion, the figures were coded for the completeness of the body as full figures or as partial figures. It was found that, of the sexually abused group, 33% drew full figures and 67% drew partial figures, suggesting an avoidance of confrontation with the lower part of the body for the majority of the group. The integrity of line quality in the drawings was coded as follows: (a) bold, outlining; (b) firm, free-flowing; or (c) faint, sketchy. Faint and sketchy line quality characterized the majority (83%) of drawings completed by the sexually abused group. This suggested an experience of anxiety and insecurity as well as a lack of assertion and energy available to the youths.

The figures were also coded according to the presence or absence of color. The authors pointed out that color responses have been related to emotional impulsivity and control, spontaneity versus passivity, and especially depression. All but one of the sexually abused youths avoided using color in their drawings, suggesting possible depression. The graphic indicators of sexual anxiety included drawings of genitals or breasts, omission of body parts, legs pressed together, hidden hands, and ambiguity of sexual identification. Surprisingly, there were no significant differences between the sexually abused youths and the nonsexually abused youths for all indicators of sexual anxiety. Although there were many significant findings of this study, the authors stressed that caution should be used in generalizing any findings to the general runaway population in either Canada or the United States regarding the prevalence of sexual abuse.

Similarly, Hagood (1988) stressed that the development of more valid and contemporary projective instruments using children's drawings is essential, and that methodologically sound studies must be carried out to better understand differences in drawings of nonabused and sexually abused youths. Last, Hagood emphasized that the theoretical dilemma currently faced by mental health professionals (i.e., whether phallic images in children's artwork are normal oedipal fantasies or images reflecting actual sexual abuse) is in need of resolution.

In addition to using drawings, clinicians often use picture projective tests such as the Children's Apperception Test and the Blackey Pictures Test. These tests can generate imaginative stories and reveal specific aspects of stressful life experiences, including sexual abuse, and they can evoke a range of affective responses. According to Kempe and Kempe (1984), "From the stories the child makes up around each picture, one has a glimpse of the child's fantasy life and this usually gives important clues to conflict areas" (p. 132). An interesting offshoot of standardized picture projective tests is the use of written fables with sexually abused children. Miller and Veltkamp (1989) indicated that fables can be used as a means for children to identify with a particular situation and to generate their comprehension of the issues involved in stressful life events, including sexual abuse. One example is the Anger Fable; this determines how family members—especially the parents—handle their anger: "A Daddy frog, Mommy frog, and their baby frog live together in a small pond. One day the Daddy frog comes home very angry and upset. What does he do? What does the Mommy frog do? What does it feel like to you?" These authors have stressed that, thus far, the clinical content of the responses given to the fables has been extremely helpful in recognizing recurrent themes generated by the child.

EVALUATING A CHILD'S ALLEGATION FOR TRUTHFULNESS

The clinician needs to examine the truthfulness of verbal information given by a child during the interview process. Sink (1988) reported that such information must be considered in light of the child's developmental capability for telling the truth, and the possibility that a fabricated story is being presented as part of a custody fight. Evaluating verbal information for each of these situations is discussed in detail next.

Developmental Capacity/Lying

Parents, teachers, and clinicians know that children at all age groups can be untruthful to get out of trouble. Also, there is a long history of not believing children in child sexual abuse cases (see Salter, 1988; Thoinot & Weysse, 1911). However, Salter reported that the research literature does not support the premise that children lie about sexual victimization. For example, Jones and McGraw (1987) reported that, in a large study that reviewed 717 sexual abuse cases, only 3% were identified as being untruthful based on a set of criteria delineated by these authors. Similar low rates of untruthfulness were found by the following researchers: 6% (Peters, 1976); 5% (Horowitz, Salt, Gomes-Schwartz, & Sauzier, 1987; cited in Jones & McGraw, 1987); and 2% (Katz-Mazur, 1979). According to Salter, "the widespread belief that children lie about sexual abuse has its origins in adult fearfulness about false accusations and not in child development" (p. 238).

The more important issue, according to Salter (1988), is for the clinician to understand why, when, and how children lie based on their developmental capacity. Table 6.8 provides information related to childhood developmental characteristics and the impact these characteristics have on the possibility of a child giving a false report of sexual victimization. This information makes it clear that children do not report their fear of sexual victimization as realities. Also, it is highly unlikely for children other than adolescents to make up an incident of sexual abuse as a strategy for revenge against an adult because they are cognitively incapable of doing this. Last, Salter stated that:

> Adolescents are cognitively capable of taking such a stance, but emotionally the overwhelming thrust of development is against it, as it makes the adolescent not

Table 6.8 Developmental Characteristics and Their Impact as Related to False Reporting of Sexual Abuse

Developmental level	Characteristics	Impact
Preschool	Accurate reporters of things that touch five senses.	Would not report that they smelled things that were not there.
		Would not report that they touched things that did not exist.
		Would not report that they saw or heard things not present.
	Incapable of lying because they are angry with someone.	Would not make up a sexual abuse story to get even with an adult.
		Would not use sexual abuse charge as a strategy to get someone into trouble.
	Thin line existing between reality and fantasy.	Imagination invents the possibility yet rarely would children report their fears as reality.
Middle childhood	Reality and fantasy are firmly drawn.	What is said is not imagined or fantasized.
	Still too concrete to be a form of revenge.	Do not make up a story as a way to get even or to get someone in trouble.
	Sexual abuse is not a normal fear of children at this age.	Would not report a false incident after sexual abuse as an exaggeration of normal fear.

(Continued)

only feel different from other adolescents, but also appear different in public. It requires an adolescent to discuss explicit sexual details with strangers, e.g., policeman, lawyers, judges, at the age most difficult to do so. The self-consciousness of adolescents regarding sexuality is legendary. (p. 242)

Fabricated Stories in Custody Fights

It is not uncommon for child sexual abuse to occur or be reported during a separation or divorce process. In fact, Mian, Wehrspann, Klajner-Diamond, LeBaron, and Winder (1986) reported that incest reports are more than twice as likely to occur with separated or divorced families than with families living

Table 6.8 Developmental Characteristics and Their Impact as Related to False Reporting of Sexual Abuse (Continued)

Developmental level	Characteristics	Impact
Adolescence	Have the cognitive ability to lie because they are angry with someone.	Would make up a story of sexual abuse as a revenge strategy for a real or imagined slight.
	Are highly embarrassed to have to talk about sexuality with strangers.	Making up a sexual abuse story is rare because teenagers do not want to be different from their peers.
	Tend to avoid behavior that would lead to peer or family pressure.	Making up a story of sexual abuse would bring too much stigmatizing public attention.
		For most teens there are many other easier ways to make a point.
	Sexual abuse is not a normal fear of adolescents.	Would not report a false incident of sexual abuse due to perceived fear.

Note. From *Treating Child Sex Offenders and Victims: A Practical Guide* (pp. 238–241) by A.C. Salter, 1988, Newbury Park, CA: Sage. Copyright 1988 by Sage. Reprinted with permission.

together. Salter (1988) cited the following reasons for this occurrence: (a) a child often reports a parent for incest only after that parent has moved out of the home and the child fears retaliation less than earlier, (b) many child sexual abusers commit incest for the first time during the dissolution of a marriage due to their psychological vulnerability, (c) a spouse commits incest as an act of revenge against the divorcing spouse, and (d) the offender has been tempted to molest a child and now, under stress and with no one to watch him, the opportunity for this act increases.

Although it is unfortunate that a family separation or divorce creates the opportunity for child sexual abuse to occur, there are fabricated charges of incest that occur due to the revenge of one spouse against another. A fabricated story of incest is rare, but the clinician needs to distinguish between accurate and inaccurate reports. With this in mind, Jones and McGraw (1987) reported the following dimension for a clinician to use when making this determination: explicit detail, unique or distinguishing detail, age-appropriate words and sentence formation, a child's perspective, affect during the reporting, affective and behavioral sequelae, the progression of the abuse, secrecy, and a precocious understanding of sexuality. Table 6.9 provides the clinician with practical descriptions of these dimensions.

Table 6.9 Dimensions and Guiding Descriptions Regarding Accurate and Inaccurate Child Sexual Abuse Reports (Salter, 1988)

Dimension	Guiding description
Detail	A parent tends not to give a young child enough details to make a lie convincing.
Unique detail	Comments related to physical sensation ("it felt sticky"), odors, or tastes for various types of sexual activities are not typical of fabricated stories.
Age-appropriate words	Adults who provide their children with a fabricated story rarely explains things with the developmental language that children would use (e.g., concrete phrasing).
Affect	Affective comments are made that do not sound rehearsed.
	When interviewed, older children who gave a fabricated story may be angered by being asked for details.
	Children who have fabricated reports often do so with a lack of affect.
	When giving false reports, children do not display the sense of puzzlement that many sexual abused children have after such acts.
	Children giving false reports do not ask questions of the interviewer, which demonstrates that the children are trying to process what happened.
	Children with fabricated stories willingly repeat the story without any difficulty in talking.
	False reporters are most willing to discuss the incest with new interviewers.
Progression	An absence of a progression of the incest is usually an indication of a false charge.
Secrecy	Fabricated stories tend to have an absence of explicit instructions regarding secrecy.

ESTABLISHING A HIERARCHICAL MODEL FOR EVALUATION

A clinician is often perplexed by the many symptoms and kinds of behavior that have been reported as sequels to sexual abuse in childhood. Because of this, a hierarchical model has been proposed that will help the clinician integrate these symptoms into their evaluations of possible sexual abuse. The model developed by Sink (1988) concerns decision making about the certainty that abuse has occurred and about recommendations for ongoing work with a child who may have been an abuse victim. The model contains four levels, with the most certainty for abuse present at Level 1 and the least at Level 4.

Level 1 Is Direct Communication

At this level, children are able to clearly and directly communicate about abusive events. They are able to give detailed, verbal accounts in age-appropriate language. Sink (1988) stressed that younger children with less verbal ability frequently demonstrate explicit sexual acts with sexually anatomically correct dolls in a structured interview format. In some cases, there are obvious signs of physical abuse.

Level 2 Is Indirect Communication

Sink (1988) stressed that a child's indirect communication about sexual abuse is not acceptable by legal standards, but can be helpful to diagnosticians. This information can be suggestive of abuse, as when a child makes ambiguous, contextual statements without going on to disclose abuse. According to Sink, the information can be as obvious as adding genitalia to man figure drawings, or as subtle as preoccupation with sexuality and secrecy.

Level 3 Is Acute Traumatic Symptomatology

These children have symptoms that reflect more general posttraumatic stress, often without specific sexualized elements. Their behavior communicates fear, anxiety, and regression in functioning. Sink (1988) emphasized that the symptomatology at Level 3 is most severe in children whose abuse was dominated by dangerous, terrorizing elements that accentuated their loss of control, the potential for harm, and panic about whether they would survive.

Level 4 Is Cumulative Stress Symptomatology

In some cases, acute posttraumatic stress following unresolved abuse evolves over time into chronic symptoms of phobia, psychosomatic complaints, aggression, and other conduct disorders. Symptoms discussed by Sink (1988) could be as diverse as bulimia, substance abuse, child molesting, or migraine headaches, and can be outward manifestations of efforts to contain a secret of ongoing or past abuse. Sink indicated that, in cases where the risk of abuse still exists, adolescents become symptomatic when their efforts to conceal abuse produce increasing psychological stress.

Sink (1988) concluded a discussion of her model with three recommendations concerning the evaluation of child sexual abuse. First, the clinician can utilize a hierarchical model to assess the certainty of sexual abuse. Although some of these data are not necessarily relevant by legal standards, they are relevant to clinical recommendations for further evaluation or treatment of a child. Second, the clinician must be trained to recognize situations not immediately amenable to direct questioning, as well as in techniques that are compatible with the legal system. Third, the clinician must be aware of timing as a central consideration in disclosure of sexual abuse.

While collecting assessment information, a number of guiding principles were emphasized in this chapter. First, clinicians need to assume that what a child says is truthful unless data occur that prove otherwise. Second, clinicians should make it as easy as possible for a child to communicate all dimensions of the sexual abuse. This can involve the use of drawings, role playing, or having the child enact what has occurred with anatomically correct dolls. Third, professionals must recognize that a child's partial or full disclosure puts him or her at risk, and, as such, clinicians should not engage in assessment behavior without providing for the child's psychological and physical safety. Last, the task of eliciting sexual abuse information from children is complex and requires a skilled clinician who can proceed without adding further psychological trauma. The hierarchical evaluation model discussed herein can be used by the clinician to prioritize assessment information.

SUMMARY

Child sexual abuse is not a new phenomenon; its occurrence has been reported throughout history. However, "the sexual revolution of the 1960's and 1970's created an atmosphere in which adults who had been sexually victimized as children were encouraged to discuss their experiences, and gradually, public awareness of the problem increased . . . and the public quickly realized that child sexual abuse was a serious social problem" (Wurtele & Miller-Perrin, 1992, p. 3). This awareness resulted in efforts to prevent and treat childhood sexual abuse, as well as systematically evaluate child sexual abuse cases.

The process of addressing childhood sexual abuse begins, as did this book, with definitions and explanations of terms and variables related to abuse, statistics on occurrence, and identification of data collection methods for gathering additional information. Children's social reasoning about adults was identified as a source of childhood vulnerability to sexual abuse, with the report of the Burkhardt study offering support for the premise that many children would have difficulty responding to a perpetrator. A child-generated model of sexual abuse intervention provides guidelines, from the child's perspective, for understanding how children respond to a perpetrator in terms of recognizing, resisting, and reporting sexually abusive encounters. Adults committed to providing, preserving, and promoting safety and wellness for all children are challenged to prevent, assess, and treat childhood sexual abuse with realistic and sensitive approaches that reflect adults' understanding of what it means to a child to encounter a perpetrator.

Appendix

The following child sexual abuse prevention materials are reviewed with particular attention paid to the issues raised by the child-generated model:

1 Do the materials take into account a range of cognitive abilities by presenting information on different levels dependent on the child's age?

2 Do the materials provide information identifying perpetrators as family and friends, as well as strangers?

3 Do the materials address the areas of recognizing, resisting, and reporting abuse?

BOOKS

Lenett, R., Barthelme, D., & Crane, B. (1986). *Sometimes it's O.K. to tell secrets!* New York: Tom Doherty Associates.

Lenett, R., & Crane, B. (1985). *It's O.K. to say no!* New York: Tom Doherty Associates.

Both of these books are meant as a parent–child manual for protection. They stress the importance of open communication between parent and child, teaching the child how to protect him- or herself when alone or with friends, and permitting the child to appear rude or impolite if he or she is in an uncomfortable or frightening situation with an adult. Although there are references to touching private parts of the body, the focus is on keeping the child safe in all situations, not just sexual ones. If the child can identify an uncomfortable situation early, he or she can hopefully avoid a sexual situation.

The guidelines for parents and the vignettes to be read with the child are aimed at children old enough to be out in the neighborhood by themselves. The vignettes describe a child in an uncomfortable situation (being asked to come into a neighbor's house, being offered money by a stranger or acquaintance, being approached by a stranger) who responds correctly: leaving and telling his or her parents what happened. The child is then asked what he or she would do in the same situation. Hopefully, the child will give the same response. If not, parents know that they must go over the information again, trying different words and examples. It should be pointed out that the parent also responds properly to the child's report: They believe the child, praise the reporting behavior, and deal with the other adult directly.

Neither of these books gives age-appropriate ways to explain the rules and guidelines to children. It is up to the adult to determine what points to stress and how to present them. There is material about both strangers and people known to the child (coach, neighbor, baby-sitter, and teacher). However, each book has one incident about a family member (uncle and stepfather).

The point of these books is for the child to recognize a problematic situation, say ''no'' and leave the area, and report the incident to his or her parents. Some situations are not inherently dangerous (e.g., neighbor asks child to come into house while he or she gets dish to return to parent), but in each one the child responds correctly (e.g., waits in front of the house for the neighbor to retrieve the dish, not entering the house) and reports to the parent. In essence, the child is told the correct and safe response before he or she is asked ''what would you do?''

Kraizer, S. (1985). *The safe child book.* New York: Dell Publishing Co.

The basis of this book is that children are capable of thinking for themselves if trained, and thinking children are safe children because parents cannot be with their children 24 hours a day. The author asserts that this training can begin as early as 3 and 4 years of age, as children naturally begin asserting their independence. The approach emphasizes preparing children for situations without using scare tactics.

Techniques include the ''what-if game,'' which can deal with topics as innocent as ''What if I spill my milk?'' to situations such as ''What if I'm home alone and I hear a funny noise?'' or ''What if I get lost in the store?'' Children participate in this game naturally, which allows the adult and child to discuss different possible behaviors and their possible consequences. Whenever possible, the child should generate the answers, thereby alerting the adult to any misinformation the child may possess.

Another instruction to children is the ''arm's reach plus'' rule. Children should be instructed to keep a distance of the adult's arm length plus some room from a stranger. They then learn to back up and run to wherever their parent is for protection. Along with this come the rules of not talking to strangers, not taking anything from a stranger (necessitating getting closer than arm's reach), and not going anywhere with a stranger. A point to be made to the children is to not even take something of their own from a stranger (e.g., a doll or ball). This concept can be difficult for even older children.

To prepare children for problematic situations, adults must allow children to voice their dislikes and concerns, even those that seem socially inappropriate. Children must learn that their feelings and instincts are as valuable as adults'. Consequently, if they do not want to kiss Grandma good-bye, they should not have to, and they should not be made to feel guilty about not doing it. This rule even extends to touching by parents. If children say they do not like to be kissed, hugged, and so on, parents must respect these wishes.

One primary message is that adults take care of children; if children are alone, they need to take care of themselves and not worry about taking care of an adult, even to the point of appearing rude.

Kraizer gives examples in the "what-if game" and "arm's reach plus" rule for children ages 3–6 years, 7–9 years, and 10–14 years. At other times, she refers to one of the age groups specifically. As stated earlier, she believes that children as young as 3 can begin learning how to protect themselves.

Although the book contains two chapters devoted to stranger issues, there is also emphasis on children's right to comfort with those they know. The point is made that most incidents of sexual abuse involve someone the child knows and trusts.

By asserting that children must learn to trust their instincts and not worry about taking care of adults, the recognition aspect is addressed. Rules such as arm's reach address the resisting aspect. The reporting aspect is couched in open communication, which can begin with the "what-if game" and be expanded with respecting the child's instincts and dislikes. If these types of situations have been discussed in a nonfrightening manner, the child should be able to easily report any occurrences.

MOVIE

Strong kids, safe kids. Paramount Pictures Inc.

This film is to be viewed by parents and children, and can be obtained at video stores (some dispense it as a free, community service video). This video is based on the Children's Self-Help Project, San Francisco, and its aim is to "prevent sexual abuse and abduction." The film constantly shifts between addressing the children and addressing the adults, so it may be difficult for children to follow. Different television personalities (e.g., "the Fonz" and John Ritter) are joined by various cartoon characters (e.g., Fred Flintstone, Scooby Doo, the Smurfs), and points are punctuated with original songs.

A major point covered in the video is building bridges between parents and children with words, with the goal of the adult being an "askable parent." There is a focus on private parts (calling them by their proper names) and the three kinds of touch (Heart—good feeling touch, No—bad feeling touch, and ?—touch that starts okay, but becomes uncomfortable). The importance of telling trustworthy adults and not keeping secrets is repeated, as is the need for children to tell someone if something happens to them, despite their efforts to protect themselves. "No, Go, and Tell" is a catch phrase.

The "Big No" is presented to children as a measure of protection—one that is only to be used when in danger, not when told to do chores, homework, and so on. The point is made that you may even need to use the "Big No" with people you know and love. The "Honk" is also introduced as a protective weapon. The child is supposed to make a deep, foghorn type sound when in danger. This is to be differentiated from children's normally high squeals, which indicate play.

The video also reveals various tricks that perpetrators may use to get a child to go with them (e.g., lost dog, candy, policeman, mom sick), as well as threats that perpetrators may use to keep the abuse a secret (e.g., parents won't love you anymore, hurt you or your family).

In addressing parents, the video stresses the importance of believing the child; it states that, although an occasional child may make up a story about sexual contact, this is not an area most children know anything about unless it really happened to them. In addition to belief, adult needs to remain calm and stress that the child is not to blame for any abuse.

It is difficult to tell exactly to which age bracket this film is directed. The songs and cartoon characters indicate a preschool level, while some of the words used appear directed toward an older age. Host Henry Winkler states that this video should be viewed many times with parents, other family members, and friends. As such, children could view this for many years, not understanding some concepts until they are older.

Much of the video is geared toward protecting children from strangers, but there are references to the possibility that someone a child knows and likes may hurt him or her with no indication of relationship.

The "No, Go, and Tell" phrase relates to recognition, resistance, and reporting. The recognition is primarily based on the protection of private parts and listening to one's inner voice about the type of touch. Resistance is addressed by the "Big No" and the "Honk." Also, children are advised repeatedly to get away from the adult as quickly as possible and report the incident to their parents.

PROGRAMS

Child Assault Prevention (CAP), 606 Delsea Drive, Sewell, New Jersey 08080; (800) 258-3189.

The CAP program is designed to make children aware of physical, sexual, and psychological abuse, as well as neglect. The presentation is through both audiovisual materials and role playing. When the children role play a situation, they are asked to identify feelings and come up with alternatives that might have better protected them in problematic situations (e.g., keep your distance, stop conversation, and walk away). The program is presented in schools for 1–4 days. Training sessions in the CAP model are available throughout the country under the direction of the national office.

The CAP program is divided into four age groups: preschool (3–5), kindergarten (5–6), elementary (first through sixth grade), and high school (seventh grade and up). The same issues are discussed, with the presentation varying according to developmental abilities. Although there is a special section on strangers (exactly who is a stranger?), the program also deals with abuse by someone known to the child. Recognition is addressed through role playing, assisting children to explore their feelings in problematic situations. Recognition is also addressed by explaining the various types of abuse and neglect. As a form of resistance, the children are taught the CAP Safety Yell, which is a low, guttural sound emanating from the diaphragm, to call attention to themselves in a dangerous situation. Adults would recognize this as an unusual sound for a child to make and come to investigate. Children are helped to identify what adults they could tell if they are abused—parents, teachers, principals—and are warned that they may not be believed by the first person whom they tell.

Empower, Big Brothers/Big Sisters, 230 North 13th Street, Philadelphia, Pennsylvania 19107; (215) 567-7000.

This program was developed for the Big Brothers/Big Sisters organization and is required of all children before they are matched with an adult. The program is run by the organization's case workers and is available to other professionals through the national office. There is also a program for parents that is considered important for providing children with an atmosphere conducive to talking about any problematic situations.

The program is for children ages 6–14, prime ages in which children enter the Big Brothers/Big Sisters program. Some agencies run the children together in one group, which lasts about 1 hour; others separate them out by age. But any individuation to age is done by the case worker dependent on the children's needs. The program addresses both stranger and known adult involvement in abuse. The program first deals with all kinds of feelings in order to help the children learn to trust their own, special feelings. They then talk about touch, both okay and not okay, and discuss the indicators of stress. If the children can learn to trust their instincts, they will be more assertive in resisting. They are told that sometimes it is all right to be rude to an adult. They utilize the "No, Go, Tell" phrase. In terms of reporting, they are advised to go to someone they trust, preferably an adult. They discuss the community of people who could fit that category. The point is made that if this happens to them once or many times, it is not their fault.

You Are Special, YWCA Sexual Assault Project, 353 E. Michigan, Kalamazoo, Michigan 49007; (616) 345-9412.

This is a 30–60-minute program that can be run by trained volunteers for children from preschool to sixth grade. The length of the program is dependent on the children's ages. There are two age categories: preschool to third grade, and fourth to sixth grade. The younger version has songs to keep the children's attention, and the older version gives more detail about problematic situations. The program deals with problematic touches and, as such, includes anyone who touches the children in a way that they "don't like." The program utilizes the "No, Go, Tell" phrase, and teaches the children to resist problematic touches, leave the situation, and go tell an adult.

Safe and Free and *Touch*, Imagination Theater, Inc., 1801 West Byron, Studio 25, Chicago, Illinois 60613; (312) 929-4100.

These programs are presented in a theater format using audience participation. *Safe and Free* is for children ages 3–6, and *Touch* is for children in kindergarten through sixth grade. There is also a presentation, "No Easy Answers," for children in seventh grade through high school. The focus is on personal body safety. The actors present situations and request suggestions from the children as to how to deal with the problems. The suggestions are then incorporated into the scene. A trained therapist acts as moderator to the play, and is available to the children in a Safe Room following the presentation if a child needs someone to talk with about an abuse problem. There is also a mandatory parent–teacher workshop prior to the presentation. The presentation is about 30 minutes long.

As noted, there are three different age groupings for the presentation, with some overlap between *Safe and Free* and *Touch*. With the younger children, the term *uh-oh feelings* is used to describe problematic touches. The program emphasizes the empowerment of the children no matter who is doing the touching—friend or stranger. The children are told to go with their instincts about whether something is okay or not, and to recognize those "uh-oh" feelings. They then practice shouting "No!" and raising their hand in a stop posture. After saying "No," the children should get away as fast as possible and find an adult to tell. Different possibilities of whom to tell are discussed.

References

Abel, G. G., Becker, J. V., Mittelman, M., Cunningham-Rathner, J., Rouleau, J. L., & Murphy, W.D. (1987). Self-reported sex crimes of nonincarcerated paraphiliacs. *Journal of Interpersonal Violence, 2*, 3–25.

Abrahams, N., Casey, K., & Daro, D. (1992). Teacher's knowledge, attitudes, and beliefs about child abuse and its prevention. *Child Abuse & Neglect, 16*, 229–238.

Adams, E. M., & Betz, N. E. (1993). Gender differences in counselors' attitudes toward and attribution about incest. *Journal of Counseling Psychology, 40*(2), 210–216.

American Psychiatric Association. (1994). *The diagnostic and statistical manual of mental disorders* (4th ed.). Washington, DC: Author.

Armstrong, L. (1978). *Kiss daddy goodnight*. New York: Hawthorne.

Askwith, J. (1982). Sex in the family. In B. Schlesinger (Ed.), *Sexual abuse of children* (pp. 52–70). Toronto: University of Toronto Press.

Baker, A. W., & Duncan, S. P. (1985). Child sexual abuse: A study of prevalence in Great Britain. *Child Abuse & Neglect, 9*, 457–467.

Banning, A. (1989). Mother-son incest: Confronting a prejudice. *Child Abuse & Neglect, 13*, 563–570.

Bass, E., & Davis, L. (1988). *The courage to heal: A guide for women survivors of child sexual abuse*. New York: Harper & Row.

Bass, E., & Davis, L. (1993). *Beginning to heal: A first book for survivors of child sexual abuse*. New York: HarperCollins.

Basta, S. M., & Peterson, R. F. (1990). Perpetrator status and the personality characteristics of molested children. *Child Abuse & Neglect, 14*, 555–566.

Berger, E. H. (1981). *Parents as partners in education: The school and home working together*. St. Louis: Mosby.

Bliss, E. L. (1984). A symptom profile of patients with multiple personality, including MMPI results. *Journal of Nervous and Mental Disorders, 172*, 197–202.

Bogat, G. A., & McGrath, M. (1993). Preschoolers' cognitions of authority, and its relationship to sexual abuse education. *Child Abuse & Neglect, 17*, 651–662.

Bolton, F. G., Morris, L. A., & MacEachron, A. E. (1989). *Males at risk*. Newbury Park, CA: Sage.

Briere, J., & Zaidi, L. Y. (1989). Sexual abuse histories in female psychiatric emergency room patients. *American Journal of Psychiatry, 146*, 1602–1606.

Brownmiller, S. (1975). *Against our will*. New York: Simon & Schuster.

Bruss-Saunders, E. (1979). *Children's thoughts about parents: A developmental study*. Unpublished doctoral dissertation, Harvard University, Cambridge, MA.

Bryer, J. B., Nelson, B. A., Miller, J. B., & Krol, P. A. (1987). Childhood sexual and physical abuse as factors in adult psychiatric illness. *American Journal of Psychiatry, 144*, 1426–1430.

Budin, L. E., & Johnson, C. F. (1989). Sex abuse prevention programs: Offenders' attitudes about their efficacy. *Child Abuse & Neglect, 13*, 77–87.

Bugental, D. B., Kopeikin, H., & Lazowski, L. (1992). Children's responses to authentic versus polite smiles. In K. J. Rotenberg (Ed.), *Children's interpersonal trust: Sensitivity to lying, deception, and promise violations* (pp. 58–79). New York: Springer-Verlag.

Burkhardt, S. (1986). *Preventing inappropriate child-stranger interactions: A comparison of three training methods*. Unpublished master's thesis, DePaul University, Chicago, IL.

Burkhardt, S. (1991). *Vulnerability to child sexual abuse as a function of level of social reasoning*. Doctoral dissertation, DePaul University, Chicago, IL.

Burton, L. (1968). *Vulnerable children*. London: Routledge & Kegan Paul.

Cantwell, H. B. (1981). Sexual abuse of children in Denver, 1979; Reviewed with implications for pediatric intervention and possible prevention. *Child Abuse & Neglect, 5*, 75–85.

Carroll, C. A., & Van Dornick, W. (1984). Data collection sexual abuse record. In R. S. Kempe & C. H. Kempe (Eds.), *The common secret: Sexual abuse of children and adolescents* (pp. 224–251). New York: W.H. Freeman.

Conte, J. R. (1986). Sexual abuse and the family: A critical analysis. *Journal of Psychotherapy and the Family, 2*(2), 113–126.

Coons, P. M., Bowman, E. S., Pellow, T. A., & Schneider, P. (1989). Post-traumatic aspects of the treatment of victims of sexual abuse and incest. *Psychiatric Clinics of North America, 12*, 325–335.

Coons, P. M., & Milstein, V. (1986). Psychosexual disturbances in multiple personality: Characteristics, etiology, and treatment. *Journal of Clinical Psychiatry, 47*, 106–110.

Corwin, D. L. (1988). Early diagnosis of child sexual abuse: Diminishing the lasting effects. In G. Wyatt & G. Powell (Eds.), *Lasting effects of child sexual abuse* (pp. 251–269). Beverly Hills, CA: Sage.

Dacey, J., & Kenny, M. (1994). *Adolescent development*. Dubuque, IA: WCB Brown & Benchmark.

Damon, W. (1977). *The social world of the child*. San Francisco: Jossey-Bass.

Darley, J., Glucksberg, S., Kamin, L., & Kinchla, R. (1981). *Psychology*. Englewood Cliffs, NJ: Prentice-Hall.

Daro, D. (1991). Child sexual abuse prevention: Separating fact from fiction. *Child Abuse & Neglect, 15*, 1–4.

Daro, D., & McCurdy, K. (1991). *Current trends in child abuse reporting and fatalities: The results of the 1990 annual fifty state survey* (Working Paper No. 808). Chicago: National Center on Child Abuse Prevention Research, National Committee for Prevention of Child Abuse.

Dayee, F. S. (1982). *Private zone*. New York: Warner Books.

Dell, P. F., & Eisenhower, J. W. (1990). Adolescent multiple personality disorder: A preliminary study of eleven cases. *Journal of the American Academy of Child and Adolescent Psychiatry, 29*, 359–366.

Deutsch, H. (1973). *The psychology of women*. New York: Bantam Books.

DeVries, R. (1969). Constancy of generic identity in the years 3 to 6. *Monographs of the Society for Research in Child Development, 34* (11, Serial No. 127).

Drossman, D. A., Leserman, J., Nachman, G., Li, Z., Gluck, H., Toomey, T. C., & Mitchell, C. M. (1990). Sexual and physical abuse in women with functional or organic gastrointestinal disorders. *Annals of Internal Medicine, 113*, 828–833.

Elkind, D. (1967). Egocentrism in adolescence. *Child Development, 38*, 1025–1034.

Faller, K. C. (1989). Characteristics of a clinical sample of sexually abused children: How boy and girl victims differ. *Child Abuse & Nelgect, 13*, 281–291.

Felner, R. D., Jason, L. A., Moritsugu, J., & Farber, S. S. (1983). *Preventive psychology: Theory, research and practice*. New York: Pergamon.

Finkelhor, D. (1979). *Sexually victimized children*. New York: The Free Press.

Finkelhor, D. (1984). *Child sexual abuse*. New York: The Free Press.

Finkelhor, D. (1986). Sexual abuse: Beyond the family systems approach. *Journal of Psychotherapy and the Family, 2*(2), 53–65.

Finkelhor, D., & Browne, A. (1986). Initial and long-term effects: A conceptual framework. In D. Finkelhor (Ed.), *A sourcebook on child sexual abuse: New theory and research*. Beverly Hills, CA: Sage.

Finkelhor, D., & Dziuba-Leatherman, J. (1994). Victimization of children. *American Psychologist, 49*(3), 173–183.

Finkelhor, D., Gelles, R., Hotaling, G., & Straus, M. (Eds.). (1983). *The dark side of families: Current family violence research* (pp. 65–81). Beverly Hills, CA: Sage.

Finkelhor, D., Hotaling, G., Lewis, I. A., & Smith, C. (1990). Sexual abuse in a national survey of adult men and women: Prevalence, characteristics, and risk factors. *Child Abuse & Neglect, 14*, 19–28.

Finkelhor, D., & Strapko, N. (1992). Sexual abuse prevention education: A review of evaluation studies. In D. J. Willis, E. W. Holden, & M. Rosenberg (Eds.), *Prevention of child maltreatment: Developmental and ecological perspectives* (pp. 150–167). New York: Wiley.

Flapan, D. (1968). *Children's understanding of social interactions*. New York: Columbia University Press.

Flavell, J. (1985). *Cognitive development* (2nd ed.). Englewood Cliffs, NJ: Prentice-Hall.

Fontana, V. J. (1982). *Sexual child abuse and the medical professional*. Washington, DC: National Committee for Prevention of Child Abuse.

Freund, K., & Watson, R. J. (1992). The proportions of heterosexual and homosexual pedophiles among sex offenders against children: An exploratory study. *Journal of Sex & Marital Therapy, 18*(1), 34–43.

Friedrich, W. N., Einbender, A. J., & Luecke, W. J. (1983). Cognitive and behavioral characteristics of physically abused children. *Journal of Consulting and Clinical Psychology, 51*, 213–214.

Friedrich, W. N., Urquiza, A. J., & Beilke, R. L. (1986). Behavioral problems in sexually abused young children. *Journal of Pediatric Psychology, 11*, 47–57.

Fritz, G. S., Stoll, K., & Wagner, N. N. (1981). A comparison of males and females who were sexually molested as children. *Journal of Sex and Marital Therapy, 7*(1), 54–59.

Fromuth, M. A., & Burkhart, B. R. (1989). Long-term psychological correlates of childhood sexual abuse in two samples of college men. *Child Abuse & Neglect, 13*, 533–542.

Frude, N. (1982). The sexual nature of sexual abuse: A review of the literature. *Child Abuse and Neglect, 6*, 211–223.

Furniss, T. (1991). *The multi-professional handbook of child sexual abuse.* London: Routledge.

Gale, J., Thompson, R. J., Moran, T., & Sack, W. H. (1988). Sexual abuse in young children: Its clinical presentation and characteristic patterns. *Child Abuse & Neglect, 12*, 163–170.

Gelman, R., & Baillargeon, R. (1983). A review of Piagetian concepts. In J. H. Flavell & E. M. Markman (Eds.), *Handbook of child psychology: Cognitive development* (Vol. 3, pp. 167–230). New York: Wiley.

Gentry, C. (1978). Incestuous abuse of children: The need for an objective view. *Child Welfare, 57*, 355–364.

Giaretto, H. (1976). Humanistic treatment of father-daughter incest. In R. E. Helfer & C. H. Kempe (Eds.), *Child abuse and neglect: The family and the community* (pp. 143–158). Cambridge, MA: Ballinger.

Gibson-Ainyette, I., Templer, D., & Brown, R. (1988). Adolescent female prostitutes. *Archives of Sexual Behavior, 17*, 431–438.

Glaser, D., & Collins, C. (1987, June). *The response of non-sexually-abused children to anatomically correct dolls.* Paper presented to the Association of Child Psychology and Psychiatry, London.

Glaser, D., & Frosh, S. (1988). *Child sexual abuse.* Chicago: The Dorsey Press.

Goldstein, E. (1992). *Confabulations.* Boca Raton, FL: SIRS Books.

Goldston, S. E. (1977). Defining primary prevention. In G. W. Albee & J. M. Joffee (Eds.), *Primary prevention of psychopathology: Vol. 1. The issues* (pp. 4–25). Hanover, NH: University Press of New England.

Gomes-Schwartz, B., Horowitz, J. M., & Cardarelli, A. P. (1990). *Child sexual abuse: The initial effects.* Newbury Park, CA: Sage.

Goodwin, J., McCarty, T., & DiVasto, P. (1981). Physical and sexual abuse of the children of adult incest victims. In J. Goodwin (Ed.), *Sexual abuse, incest victims and their families* (pp. 17–26). Boston: John Wright.

Green, A. H. (1993). Child sexual abuse: Immediate and long-term effects and interventions. *Journal of the American Academy of Child and Adolescent Psychiatry, 32*(5), 890–904.

Hagood, M. M. (1988). Diagnosis or dilemma: Drawings of sexually abused children. *British Journal of Projective Psychology, 71,* 103–117.

Hall, R. C. W., Tice, L., Beresford, T. P., Wooley, B., & Hall, A. K. (1989). Sexual abuse in patients with anorexia nervosa and bulimia. *Psychosomatics, 40,* 73–79.

Harper, J. (1993). Prepuberal male victims of incest: A clinical study. *Child Abuse & Neglect, 17,* 419–421.

Hazzard, A., Webb, C., Kleemeier, C., Angert, L., & Pohl, J. (1991). Child sexual abuse prevention: Evaluation and one-year follow-up. *Child Abuse & Neglect, 15,* 123–138.

Herman, J., & Hirschman, L. (1977). Father-daughter incest. *Signs, 4,* 735–756.

Herman, J., & Hirschman, L. (1981). Families at risk for father-daughter incest. *American Journal of Psychiatry, 13,* 967–970.

Herman, J. L., Perry, J. C., & van der Kolk, B. A. (1989). Childhood trauma in borderline personality disorder. *American Journal of Psychiatry, 146,* 490–495.

Herman, J. L., & van der Kolk, B. A. (1987). Traumatic antecedents of borderline personality disorder. In B. A. van der Kolk (Ed.), *Psychological trauma* (pp. 121–140). Washington, DC: American Psychiatric Press.

Hibbard, R. A., & Hartman, G. L. (1992). Behavioral problems in alleged sexual abuse victims. *Child Abuse & Neglect, 16,* 755–762.

Hoffman, L., Paris, S., Hall, E., & Schell, R. (1988). *Developmental psychology today* (5th ed.). New York: Random House.

Howe, J. W., Burgess, A. W., & McCormack, A. (1987, Spring). Adolescent runaways and their drawings: Special Issue. Childhood sexual abuse. *Arts in Psychotherapy, 50,* 80–88.

Inhelder, B., & Piaget, J. (1958). *The growth of logical thinking from childhood to adolescence.* New York: Basic Books.

Jacobson, A., & Herald, C. (1990). The relevance of childhood sexual abuse to adult psychiatric inpatient care. *Hospital and Community Psychiatry, 41,* 154–158.

Johnson, B., & Morse, H. (1968). Injured children and their parents. *Children, 15,* 147–152.

Jones, D. P. H., & McGraw, J. M. (1987). Reliable and fictitious accounts of sexual abuse to children. *Journal of Interpersonal Violence, 2,* 27–45.

Justice, B., & Justice, R. (1979). *The broken taboo: Sex in the family.* New York: Human Sciences Press.

Kaplan, H. I., & Sadock, B. J. (1991). *Synopsis of psychiatry: Behavioral sciences, clinical psychiatry* (6th ed.). Baltimore, MD: Williams & Wilkins.

Katz, S., & Mazur, M. A. (1979). *Understanding the rape victim: A synthesis of research findings.* New York: Wiley.

Kemper, R. S., & Kempe, C. H. (1984). *The common secret: Sexual abuse of children and adolescents.* New York: W.H. Freeman.

Kerns, D. L., & Ritter, M. L. (1991, September). *Data analysis of the medical evaluation of 1,800 suspected child sexual abuse victims.* Paper presented at the ninth national conference on Child Abuse and Neglect, Denver, CO.

Kinsey, A. C., Pomeroy, W. B., Martin, C. E., & Gebhard, P. H. (1953). *Sexual behavior in human females.* Philadelphia: W. B. Saunders.

Kohlberg, L. (1976). Moral stages and moralization: The cognitive-developmental approach. In T. Lickona (Ed.), *Moral development and behavior: Theory, research, and social issues* (pp. 30–52). New York: Holt, Rinehart & Winston.

Kraizer, S. K. (1985). *The safe child book*. New York: Dell Publishing.

Langevin, R., Day, D., Handy, L., & Russon, A. (1985). Are incestuous fathers pedophiliac, aggressive and alcoholic? In R. Langevin (Ed.), *Erotic preferences, gender identity and aggression in men* (pp. 64–90). Hillsdale, NJ: Lawrence Erlbaum Associates.

Larson, N. R., & Maddock, J. W. (1986). Structural and functional variables in incest family systems: Implications for assessment and treatment. *Journal of Psychotherapy and the Family*, 2(2), 27–44.

Lawson, C. (1993). Mother-son sexual abuse: Rare or underreported? A critique of the research. *Child Abuse & Neglect, 17*, 261–269.

Lenett, R. (1985). *It's OK to say no!* New York: Tom Koherty Associates.

Madak, P. R., & Berg, D. H. (1992). The prevention of sexual abuse: An evaluation of "Talking about Touching." *Canadian Journal of Counseling*, 26(1), 29–40.

Malcolm, J. (1983). *In the Freud archives*. New York: Alfred A. Knopf.

Mannarino, A. P., Cohen, J. A., & Berman, S. R. (1994). The relationship between preabuse factors and psychological symptomatology in sexually abused girls. *Child Abuse & Neglect, 18*, 63–71.

Masson, J. M. (1984). *The assault on truth: Freud's suppression of the seduction theory*. New York: Farrar, Straus & Giroux.

McCall, C. (1984, December). The cruelest crime. *Life*, pp. 35–62.

McCoy, D. L. (1987). *Sexual Abuse Screening Inventory*. Minneapolis: Magic Lantern Publications.

Melton, G. B. (1992a). The improbability of prevention of sexual abuse. In D. J. Willis, E. W. Holden, & M. Rosenberg (Eds.), *Prevention of child maltreatment: Developmental and ecological perspectives* (pp. 168–189). New York: Wiley.

Melton, G. B. (1992b). Foreword. In S. K. Wurtele & C. L. Miller-Perrin (Eds.), *Preventing child sexual abuse: Sharing the responsibility*. Lincoln, NE: University of Nebraska Press.

Mian, M., Wehrspann, W., Klajner-Diamond, H., LeBaron, D., & Winder, C. (1986). Review of 125 children 6 years of age and under who were sexually abused. *Child Abuse & Neglect, 10*, 223–229.

Mrazek, D. A., & Mrazek, P. B. (1981). Psychosexual development within the family. In P. B. Mrazek & C. H. Kempe (Eds.), *Sexually abused children and their families* (pp. 80–98). New York: Pergamon.

National Center on Child Abuse and Neglect. (1978). *Special Report Child Sexual Abuse: Incest assault and sexual exploitation* (DHHS Pub. No. OHDS 79-30166). Washington, DC: Author.

Neilson, T. (1983). Sexual abuse of boys: Current perspectives. *The Personnel and Guidance Journal, 62*, 139–142.

Newman, S. (1985). *Never say yes to a stranger*. New York: Putnam.

Nisbett, R., & Ross, L. (1980). *Human inferences: Strategies and shortcomings of social judgement*. Englewood Cliffs, NJ: Prentice-Hall.

Olafson, E., Corwin, D. L., & Summit, R. C. (1993). Modern history of child sexual abuse awareness: Cycles of discovery and suppression. *Child Abuse & Neglect, 17*, 7–24.

Paddison, P. L., Gise, L. H., Lebovits, A., Strain, J. J., Cirasole, D. M., & Levine, J. P. (1990). Sexual abuse and premenstrual syndrome: Comparison between a lower and higher socioeconomic group. *Psychosomatics, 31*, 265–272.

Peake, A. (1989). Issue of under-reporting. The sexual abuse of boys. *Educational and Child Psychology, 6,* 42–50.

Pelcovitz, D., Adler, N. A., Kaplan, S., Packman, L., & Krieger, R. (1992). The failure of a school-based child sexual abuse prevention program. *Journal of the American Academy of Child and Adolescent Psychiatry, 31*(5), 887–892.

Peters, J. J. (1976). Children who are victims of sexual assault and the psychology of offenders. *American Journal of Psychotherapy, 30,* 398–421.

Peters, S., Wyatt, G., & Finkelhor, D. (1986). Prevalence. In D. Finkelhor (Ed.), *Sourcebook on child sexual abuse* (pp. 90–105). Newbury Park, CA: Sage.

Piaget, J. (1970). Piaget's theory. In P. H. Mussen (Ed.), *Carmichael's manual of child psychology* (3rd ed., Vol. 1, pp. 240–255). New York: Wiley.

Plummer, C. A. (1984). *Preventing sexual abuse: Activities and strategies for those working with children and adolescents.* Holmes Beach, FL: Learning Publications.

Poston, C., & Lison, K. (1989). *Reclaiming our lives.* Boston: Little, Brown.

Powers, J., & Eckenrode, J. (1992, March). *The epidemiology of adolescent maltreatment.* Paper presented at the fourth biennial meeting of the Society for Research on Adolescence, Washington, DC.

Rew, L., & Esparza, D. (1990). Barriers to disclosure among sexually abused male children. *Journal of Child and Adolescent Psychiatric and Mental Health Nursing, 3,* 120–127.

Rohsenow, D. J., Corbett, R., & Devine, D. (1988). Molested as children: A hidden contribution to substance abuse? *Journal of Substance Abuse Treatment, 5,* 13–18.

Rotatori, A. F., & Day, G. (1990). Assessing the abused student. In A. F. Rotatori, R. A. Fox, D. Sexton, & J. Miller (Eds.), *Comprehensive assessment in special education: Approaches, procedures, and concerns* (pp. 420–437). Springfield, IL: Charles C Thomas.

Rotatori, A. F., Steckler, S., Fox, R. A., & Green, H. (1984). A multidisciplinary approach to assessing the abused youngster. *Early Child Development and Care, 14,* 93–108.

Rotenberg, K. J. (1991). Children's interpersonal trust: An introduction. In K. J. Rotenberg (Ed.), *Children's interpersonal trust: Sensitivity to lying, deception, and promise violations* (pp. 1–4). New York: Springer-Verlag.

Rush, F. (1980). *The best kept secret: Sexual abuse of children.* Englewood Cliffs, NJ: Prentice-Hall.

Russell, D. (1984). *Sexual exploitation: Rape, child sexual abuse, and sexual harassment.* Beverly Hills, CA: Sage.

Russell, D. E. H. (1983). The incidence and prevalence of intrafamilial and extrafamilial sexual abuse of female children. *Child Abuse & Neglect, 7,* 133–146.

Salter, A. C. (1988). *Treating child sex offenders and victims: A practical guide.* Newbury Park, CA: Sage.

Sarason, I. G., & Sarason, B. R. (1984). *Abnormal psychology: The problem of maladaptive behavior* (4th ed.). Englewood Cliffs, NJ: Prentice-Hall.

Saunders, B. E., Villeponteaux, L. A., Lipovsky, J. A., Kilpatrick, D. G., & Veronen, L. J. (1992). Child sexual assault as a risk factor for mental disorders among women: A community survey. *Journal of Interpersonal Violence, 7,* 189–204.

Schechter, M., & Roberge, L. (1976). Child sexual abuse. In R. Helter & C. Kempe (Eds.), *Child abuse and neglect: The family and the community* (pp. 111–130). Cambridge, MA: Ballinger.

Scott, K. D. (1992). Childhood sexual abuse: Impact on a community's mental health status. *Child Abuse & Neglect, 16*, 284–295.

Sedlak, A. J. (1991). *Supplementary analyses of data on the national incidence of child abuse and neglect.* Rockville, MD: Westat.

Selman, R. (1980). *The growth of interpersonal understanding.* New York: Academic Press.

Selman, R., Jaquette, D., & Bruss-Saunders, E. (1979). *Assessing interpersonal understanding: An interview and scoring manual.* Cambridge, MA: Judge Baker Social Reasoning Project.

Shamroy, J. (1982). A perspective on childhood sexual abuse. In S. Antler (Ed.), *Child abuse and child protection: Policy and practice* (pp. 110–113). Silver Spring, MD: National Association of Special Workers.

Shantz, C. U. (1975). The development of social cognition. In E. M. Hetherington (Ed.), *Review of child development research* (Vol. 5, pp. 90–122). Chicago: University of Chicago Press.

Siegel, J. M., Sorenson, S. B., Golding, J. M., Burnam, M. A., & Stein, J. A. (1987). The prevalence of childhood sexual assault: The Los Angeles epidemiologic catchment area project. *American Journal of Epidemiology, 126*, 1141–1153.

Siegler, R. S. (1983). Information processing approaches to cognitive development. In W. Kessen (Ed.), *Handbook of child psychology: History, theory, and methods* (Vol. 1, pp. 74–112). New York: Wiley.

Sink, F. (1988). A hierarchical model for evaluation of child sexual abuse. *American Journal of Orthopsychiatry, 58*, 246–256.

Solnit, A., Nordhaus, B., & Lard, R. (1992). *When home is no haven.* New Haven, CT: Yale University Press.

Sternberg, R. J., & Powell, J. S. (1983). The development of intelligence. In J. H. Flavell & E. M. Markman (Eds.), *Handbook of child psychology: Cognitive development* (Vol. 3, pp. 341–419). New York: Wiley.

Strauss, M. (1973). A general systems theory approach to a theory of violence between family members. *Social Science Information, 12*, 105–125.

Summit, R. (1983). The sexual abuse accommodation syndrome. *Child Abuse & Neglect, 7*, 177–193.

Terr, L. C. (1991). Childhood traumas: An outline and overview. *American Journal of Psychiatry, 148*, 10–20.

Thoinot, L., & Weysse, A. W. (1911). *Medicolegal aspects of moral offenses.* Philadelphia: F. A. Davis.

Tierney, K., & Corwin, D. (1983). Exploring intra-familial sexual abuse: A systems approach. In D. Finkelhor, R. Gelles, G. Hotaling, & M. Straus (Eds.), *The dark side of families: Current family violence research* (pp. 102–116). Beverly Hills, CA: Sage.

Trepper, T. S., & Barrett, M. J. (1986). Treating incest: A multimodal systems perspective. *Journal of Psychology and the Family, 2*(2), 5–12.

Tutty, L. (1991). Child sexual abuse: A range of prevention options [Special Issue]. *Journal of Child and Youth Care, 25*, 23–41.

Tutty, L. M. (1994). Developmental issues in young children's learning of sexual abuse prevention concepts. *Child Abuse & Neglect, 18*(2), 179–192.

Tversky, A., & Kahneman, D. (1973). Availability: A heuristic for judging frequency and probability. *Cognitive Psychology, 5*, 207–232.

Vander Mey, B. J. (1988). The sexual victimization of male children: A review of previous research. *Child Abuse & Neglect, 12*, 61–72.

Wellman, M. M. (1993). Child sexual abuse and gender differences: Attitudes and prevalence. *Child Abuse & Neglect, 17*, 539–547.

Western, D., Ludolph, P., Misle, B., Ruffins, S., & Block, J. (1990). Physical and sexual abuse in adolescent girls with borderline personality disorder. *American Journal of Orthopsychiatry, 60*, 55–66.

Whitcomb, D. (1992). *When the victim is a child.* Washington, DC: United States Department of Justice.

Wurtele, S. K., Kaplan, G. M., & Keairnes, M. (1990). Childhood sexual abuse among chronic pain patients. *The Clinical Journal of Pain, 6*, 110–113.

Wurtele, S. K., Kast, L. C., & Melzer, A. M. (1992). Sexual abuse prevention education for young children: A comparison of teachers and parents as instructors. *Child Abuse & Neglect, 16*, 865–876.

Wurtele, S. K., & Miller, C. L. (1987). Children's conceptions of sexual abuse. *Journal of Clinical Child Psychology, 16*(3), 184–191.

Wurtele, S. K., & Miller-Perrin, C. L. (1992). *Preventing child sexual abuse: Sharing the responsibility.* Lincoln, NE: University of Nebraska Press.

Wyatt, G. E. (1985). The sexual abuse of Afro-American and white-American women in childhood. *Child Abuse & Neglect, 9*, 507–519.

Wylie, M. S. (1993, September/October). The shadow of doubt. *The Family Therapy Networker*, pp. 18–29.

Yapko, M. (1993, September/October). The seductions of memory. *The Family Therapy Networker*, pp. 30–37.

Youniss, J. (1980). *Parents and peers in social development: A Sullivan-Piaget perspective.* Chicago: University of Chicago Press.

Index